CHURCH
PROPHETS

Paula A. Price, D.Min., Ph.D.

Flaming Vision Publications
Tulsa, Oklahoma

Unless otherwise indicated, all scriptural quotations are from the *King James Version* of the Bible.

Scripture verses marked NIV are taken from the *Holy Bible, New International Version,* ©1973, 1978, 1984 by the International Bible Society. Used by permission of Zondervan Publishing House.

Church Prophets
Published by:
Flaming Vision Publications
Tulsa, OK 74136
ISBN 1-886288-42-9

Printed in the United States of America

CHURCH PROPHETS

Paula A. Price, D.Min., Ph.D.

CONTENTS

PREFACE

God is reinstating the office of the prophet as a standing institution in the New Testament church. The pervasive rise in occult activity, coupled with the church's naiveté in spiritual matters, are two of the main reasons why He must do so. In view of His divine agenda, questions concerning the office of the prophet and its modern-day functions in the local church are on many leaders' minds. Discussions are held regularly by church officials who ask how to engage prophets in the local church without surrendering authority over their sheep and control of the church's mandate. Their questions include how they should install their church's prophetic institution and administrate it effectively. They ask, "Is there some sort of ceremony that should be held for inaugurating those who occupy the place of the church prophet?" Furthermore, they wonder if there are professional credentials for the prophet. If there are credentials to certify and authenticate them, who devises the criteria and how is the officer to be equipped to succeed? Should the church have its own prophetic training program, and if so, who delivers it?

Once the issues of installing the prophetic in the local church as an institution are resolved, the next most pertinent question becomes, what are they to do? This generation wants to know how the contemporary prophet is to be employed in their churches, and how he is to benefit and *profit* the church. That is right. According to Jeremiah 23:32, prophets exist in the houses of the Lord to profit them. That on its own is a powerful statement, because people rarely think about prophetics and profitability going hand in hand. Yet, that is what they are intended to do, based on the wording of 2 Chronicles 20:20.

Church Prophets shows how churches can multiply their harvests through a quality prophetic institution. It boldly delves into these matters and answers the questions above, and many others essential to validating prophetics today, and the officers and ministers who handle it. For the pastor who wants to know how to comply with the Lord's new and insistent prophetic move, this book can be an indispensable tool. No longer does a devoted shepherd have to choose between ignoring the imposing unction of the Lord to open their churches up to the prophetic or risk exposing their flocks to irresponsible prophets. With this book, it is now possible to evaluate the prophetic messenger(s) you engage and confirm their eligibility and compatibility with your church before they are presented to your congregations. It is suggested reading if you are a prophetic educator, minister, or trainer. In this book, you get help as a pastor in developing budding prophets, redefining the seasoned ones, and educating the congregation on the subject as a whole.

Church Prophets was compiled from a series of articles printed in a New York Christian newspaper. It frankly addresses pastor's concerns over installing prophets they feel are assigned to their congregations. With the Lord steadily advancing the prophetic in these last days, and in response to it, this book clarifies for church leaders the best way to integrate resident prophet ministries in their churches. You will find it contains sound balanced guidelines for the institution and regulation of the officer in the churches of God using His wisdom. It takes you into the world of the prophetic and shows you how the prophet's ministry and mantle are invaluable for pastors and others. You receive details on the responsibilities, duties, and privileges of prophets in the house of God.

You are provided with suggestions for compensating staff prophets, training and qualifying them for service, fine tuning their behavior, and fixing their range of authority. Also, there are guidelines for assessing prophets' performance and effectiveness, and strategies for managing difficult or untrained prophets. There is counsel for resolving conflicts with difficult prophets and how to protect your flock from them. Emerging prophets in the church who read this book can find themselves, understand what the Lord is doing with and through them, and receive guidance on how to approach and work with their pastors in their new callings. Such information is helpful to churches determined to have a quality and professional prophetic institution.

Candidly discussed are other prophet-related issues, like the godly church prophet, prophetic protocols, parameters, limits, and government. Besides these, the most critical subject of all is forthrightly treated: the relationship between the pastor and the prophet. This vital discussion encompasses advice on the boundaries to be put on the prophet's interactions with the sheep and correcting errant prophetics. It talks openly about the necessary shifts in normal prophetic authority that must take place if the congregation is to be edified by the church prophet without sacrificing the pastor's position. Covered also are how and why the pastor is not relegated to the prophet, but is urged to create a cooperative alliance between the two mantles. The common recurring theme of the book stresses the importance of quickly establishing a functional pastor-prophet relationship. It is necessary that the first link in the prophetic institution's chain of events be forged between the pastor-prophet ministry. Such requirements are vital if the arrangement is to benefit the church's vision and edify its members.

Chapter 1

OVERVIEW

Pastors wanting to fulfill the will of God on the prophetic in their churches regularly ask me how to go about it, and what criteria they are to use to do so. They want to grasp the wisdom of installing and working with a church prophet beforehand in order to protect their congregations. Generally, pastors desire some reliable tools to evaluate their prophetic ministers (past, present, and future) and guidelines that enable their proper use of the ministry in the local church. Whenever questions arise over the matter, it is not resistance I most often meet, but confusion and curiosity.

Many pastors say they would gladly comply with the Lord in His present prophetic move if they could just understand how. They are rightfully concerned about how to install church prophets without disrupting their church's order and unduly exposing their flocks to immature or incompetent prophets. They further want to understand how to set the mantle of the prophet within their existing church structure, while keeping the balance of control and power intact. Intact means not letting pastoral authority be swept out of their hands by prophetic fascination. Frankly, I agree with them and hold similar reservations when acknowledging and developing budding prophets entrusted to my care. Before all else, I emphasize the importance of knowing well the prophet's history.

Factors like the character and the ability of the minister should be thoroughly employed. Their background, prophetic track record, and relations with others, if they are not members of the congregation, should be investigated with care and discretion. Such information is helpful in gauging the potential success of prophetic candidates.

For example, it is defeating to use a prophet with less experience and expertise than the number of years the church has been in existence. It is also imprudent to use a prophet who has no heart for the sheep, whose time is spent doing anything but contributing to the nurture of the flock of God. If the pastor is the only one that arouses the prophet's responses or interest, and he or she remains unaffected by everything else related to the church, then such a person may not be a good church prophet. They may serve well as an itinerant minister brought in at strategic times in the church's progress, but they should not be trusted with long-term prophetic duties or authority. Factors like these require meticulous attention to qualify the prophets themselves and protect those with whom they work.

The underlying aim of stringent investigation is prudence. It is necessary to assure the facilitation of the prophet's ministry in the church, to enable God's unimpeded access to the ears, hearts, and minds of His people. What makes this process indispensable is its ability to curtail prophetic incompatibility and expand the presently narrow ministry field of prophetics ordained by God to this generation. Beyond that, it furnishes earnest church officials with reliable measures for their developing prophetic institutions and promotes healthy prophetic growth, maturity, and stability at the same time. In addition it protects this all-important ministry in the New Testament church.

This chapter gives you a quick overview of the essential elements of any serious prophetic discussion. It shows the important pieces of the puzzle for those seeking to learn about the prophet in God's church. As you review the pages to follow, you get a true picture of the ministry, mantle, and operations of the church in snapshot form.

Following is an overview of the material that you should study to help you connect with the discussions in this book. The topics are:

1. FAQs—Frequently Asked Questions
2. Concerning the Prophetic
3. Key Terms and Phrases
4. About God's Prophets and Prophetics
5. The Full Spectrum of the Prophetic
6. Are Prophets for Today?
7. Am I a Prophet?

What People Always Want to Know
About the Prophet and the Prophetic

If you are going to install a prophetic institution, enter the prophetic, and/or fulfill the office of the prophet, you need to be aware of the questions that lodge in peoples minds concerning it. Below are questions frequently asked concerning the prophets and prophetics of the office and the officer, dreams and visions, and the validity of the mantle's operations today. Familiarize yourself with them because the general consensus is that if one is going to prophesy and expect to be believed, they should at least be able to answer the following with clarity. Although not addressed in the listed order, you will get the answers to the questions as you go through the book. Take time to jot them down as you come upon them. Check off each one as you get the answers to it.

FAQs—Frequently Asked Questions
- What is a prophet?
- How does one become a prophet?
- How do prophets do what they do?
- If I'm not a prophet, do I still need to learn about prophetics?

- Why do we need prophets to tell us what God is saying when we have the Holy Spirit?
- How can psychics accurately tell the future?
- Are prophets really for today?
- I dream and know things in advance.
- Am I a prophet?
- Prophecy is what exactly?
- Where does prophecy come from?

God's Prophetic Sphere

The most challenging thought to grasp about the prophetic is that the office is more than a prediction center. Since prophecy is where most people usually encounter the institution of the prophetic, they presume the gist of the office is exclusively prophesying—seeing and saying, predicting and interdicting. However, many things go into enabling a prophet to be able to prophesy accurately.

What Equips the Prophet?

Before God releases the officer, He puts the prophet through an extensive training program. God's way of equipping for ministry is mainly spiritual. The prophet's function is largely supernatural, and people think there is nothing more to getting a prophet ready for the Lord's service than hearing and saying, "Thus says the Lord." For many people, prophetic preparation amounts to God isolating beginners and streaming prophetic dreams and visions at them. Truthfully, it is somewhat that way, but usually down the line a bit. Nonetheless, dreams and visions are how God presents Himself to the new prophet. The reason visions and dreams are the starting point of prophetic education is that God introduces Himself and awakens the prophet's revelatory faculties through them. See Numbers 12:6.

Once the novice prophet is made aware of the calling, the Lord's preparatory methods shift to more stringent and demanding activities. Proverbs 15:33 and 18:12 become the primary lesson objectives. Read the two short little passages to discover the Lord's teaching objectives and then relate them to 1 Peter 5:10. From your reading you can see that God diligently goes after the inherent and nurtured pride, arrogance, and independence of the young prophet since submission is the predominant requirement of prophetic service. Once this begins, things really heat up.

For a season, it may appear that prophesying is the last thing God wants of His new student. Resetting the newcomer's attitude, perspectives, and priorities to perform reliable prophetic services takes precedence over all else.

The initial classes are largely experiential, the curriculum multidimensional, and the tests excruciating. Yet the Lord finally does get His messengers ready for His service. The requisite areas of learning are spirituality, morality, integrity, discipline, and obedience. Integrated in their dynamics are ancient prophetics and history, revelatory techniques, and the scope of predictive prophecy. Trainers and mentors are selected from every area of human life, since that is the field the prophetic targets. The developing prophet encounters and interacts with every sphere of human existence so that the mantle is equipped to treat its every condition. Verbalizing may be the medium of administration, but the aims and outcomes of prophetic ministry are far more diverse.

Quick Study Chart
Prophetic Training

Following is a list of prophetic subject matter which God teaches His prophets to make sure they are competent in their positions. Review it to comprehend the rationale of God's prophetic training path for you.

Prophetic Subject Matter
- The prophetic is the second most important office in God's

supernatural branch of ministry

- The prophetic as an agency
- The prophetic as a commissioned office
- The prophet as an agent of the Godhead
- The prophetic as an agency with indelible functions in the church and the world
- The role and place of the second most important office in God's ministry
- The prophetic's agency status and authority
- The nature of a prophetic commission
- What happens when prophets become God's functionaries
- The prophetic's impact on Creator God's immutable creation codes

If I'm Not a Prophet,
Do I Still Need to Learn About Prophetics?

The answer to the question is emphatically yes! Everyone who is saved should know about the prophetic because that is how the church came into existence, and how the Lord speaks to, and through, His people. The Creator spoke His plans to have a family, a people, and a nation for Himself long before any of it came into being. Those prophetic words acted on creation every day until the vision of God's heart came to be.

Based on God's method of bringing His word to pass in our times, speaking and thereby causing what He said to come into being, prophecy apparently holds a high place in His mind. When the Lord speaks, His spiritual words encompass natural bodies, making prophecy the only way to get His eternal provisions from there to here. This is how it goes. First are the words, which are uttered outside time. From that seemingly insignificant act comes the natural body for them in time.

All that goes into making a vision a reality and materializing an idea are set in motion by this simple means. What leaves God's mouth is incubated and matured in much the same way an embryo progresses to a fetus and a fetus is born as a baby. Here is the main reason why much of what God says to and through His prophets is equated with impregnation, gestation, travailing women, and birth. The invisible process of God's word coming to pass is precisely like the visible process of conceiving and bearing a child. See Isaiah 55:11 and 61:11. Isaiah 60:22 speaks of God's words having their time, and Jeremiah 1:12 answers this with the time coinciding with His words' performance. Following are some significant words that are helpful to understanding this material. They are under the heading of "Key Terms and Phrases."

Important Prophetic Terms

Key Terms and Phrases

- Prophet
- Protocol
- Protocratic
- Prophetic Attributes
- Prophetic Authority
- Prophetic Skill
- Foundational Studies
- Functionary
- Ministry
- Prophecy
- Commission
- Prophetic Jurisdiction
- Prophetic Mantle
- Seer
- Psalmist
- Dreams

- Prophetic Studies
- Biblical Prophetics
- Prophetic Ministrations
- Features and Functions
- A Prophetic Feature
- A Prophetic Function
- Vision
- Official
- Office
- Officer
- Agent
- Agency
- Prophecy
- Divine
- Divination
- Symbols

Throughout this book you will see these terms and phrases that best define the prophetic as covered here. These terms are important for your grasp of its material and for identifying the terms applied to prophetic ministry. It is suggested that you research them on your own and get familiar with their usage in general. A brief glossary of their meanings is in the back of the book. We encourage you, as you go through the book, to refer to them again and again to apply their meanings to the prophetic office and its mantle while learning about the subject from your reading.

If you are a class, a learning group, or a prophetic study team, take time to explore these terms and their relevance to competent prophetic ministry. You can find more specific meanings and applications of these words in Dr. Paula A. Price's *Constructing the Contemporary Prophet* and *Biblical Prophetics*.

About God's Prophets and Prophetics

The list below shows you the good amount of information packed into this book. To operate as a professional prophet people can trust, you need answers to the above statements for those who inquire of God through you. This handy resource is a constant companion in your professional ministry.

- What the prophet is
- The nature of the prophetic institution
- Office/gift distinctives
- Office/vessel criteria
- Prophetic duties
- Prophetic territories
- Prophetics in the local church
- The proper prophetic lifestyle
- 21st century prophetics and how the world and the church must be prepared

To get where God needs you to be prophetically, you need to understand:

- Prophets and the church
- Prophets and the world
- Prophets vs. psychics in Christ
- Prophets of old
- Prophets today
- The proper prophetic lifestyle
- Prophetic features and functions
- 21st century prophetics and how the world and the church must be prepared

Full Prophetic Knowledge

When one thinks about the full spectrum of the prophetic, the following should come to mind:

- Native prophetic abilities born in all prophets
- Prophetic personalities that indicate the call to the office
- Supernatural attire, the invisible insignia of power and authority
- Angelic delegation
- Miracles and signs
- Prophetic dreams
- Prophetic order and protocol
- Supernatural orders
- Eternal reasons for the prophet
- Prophetic streams

Are Prophets for Today?

Prophets are as much for today as anything else that has ever been. Here are some good reasons why prophets are, and will continue to be, needed by God for some time. Revelation 11 declares they will be active until the end of this age.

- God, the devil, man, and the world are all interrelated and prophets are how each one contacts and conveys information to the other.
- It does not matter how modern we appear, closer scrutiny shows we have not progressed so far after all.
- Technology names its work after the same demons the Lord has fought with since antiquity.
- Prophets still confront the same sin in humanity that has existed since eternity.
- Television today, and the entertainment media in general, can do little without the same vulgarity that has pervaded the planet since time began.
- Sexual perversion—immorality, obscenity, homosexuality, and lewdness
- Lust
- Greed
- The devil and his children still operate in deception, delusion, sin, and perversity.

All in all, one can *say* the people of earth are still bound by the same sins that have always populated the planet. Heaven is still in control, hell still waits, Adam's seed continues to be formed, and the devil waits at their birth to claim them for his fate.

I Dream and Know Things in Advance— Am I a Prophet?

Possibly, but remember, prophets are prophets from birth. God deposited their gifts in them from eternity and developed them like the rest of their makeup over time. What constitutes their being a bona fide prophet is the prophet's spirit, discussed later. You may however be a seer. This can be so if you are an intense prayer warrior, relentless intercessor, or are highly responsive to spiritual matters. Under these circumstances the seer or intercessor can easily be mistaken for a prophet when they are not. Psalmists too have been mistakenly declared prophets. In all instances, the common denominator is unusual supernatural interactions, responses, and information. What all three cases lack is the distinct enforcement power and spiritual authority intrinsic to the prophet's mantle.

More than just *seeing and saying,* identifying and combating, or hearing and singing, the official prophet exceeds all these supernatural manifestations with powerful spiritual latitude. The prophet receives from God, upon completed training, significant license in the spiritual realm. The minister is also deployed a potent angelic guard that performs his or her words. With these, (s)he enjoys a rank in God's kingdom to compel obedience to their prophecies over time, all unlike the seer.

A seer, compared to the prophet or the others, sees things with their inner being (spiritual eyes) beyond their five senses. A seer easily bypasses the natural eyes to accurately detect what is around them in the spiritual world. This ability is not limited to time and space. If you are a seer, you may also be a dreamer of dreams, although the two can be exclusive of each other. The dreamer of dreams is similar to a seer except the information received from the spirit world is only received by dreams or in a dreamlike state. Historically this method of revelatory communication has been deemed the most unreliable form of spiritual reception. Prophetic dreams too easily mix with dreamers' emotions, personality, daily events, and life experiences and can contaminate the message's purity. However, the dream is nonetheless a valid tool of prophetic reception used by the Lord from time to time.

In the prophet, all the preceding faculties work together as one, operating either intermittently in an active prophetic environment, or randomly in specific prophetic situations. What distinguishes the prophet is the officer's interpretative, translation, and application ability that enhance their predictions and empower their faculties. Together these render their word more useful.

Chapter 2

CHURCH PROPHET IMPORTANCE

The importance of the church prophet in the church cannot be over stated in our present times. Rising occultism, witchcraft, and sorcery all create a domination of darkness in every stratum of society. Ignorance to the Creator's prophetics along with the church's resistance to the officer's reinstatement can be blamed. Add to that the church's apostate stance on critical spiritual and moral issues, and you see the conflicting duality. On one hand, these issues clearly set forth God's need for the prophet and on the other, they answer why and how prophets are shunned and relentlessly persecuted.

Still, the rising tide of demonism, looming greater than ever on the horizons of our last days, means the prophet, as God's level-two power ministry, must be raised up and equipped to confront it. To better understand this, think about the worlds of Elijah and Elisha, two renowned prophets in ancient Israel during the era of the kings. Recall the state of affairs that motivated them and you see why God's only response is prophetic reinstatement.

The light had virtually been snuffed out by paganism, and God's people no longer knew the real from the false. Their entire spiritual climate was black with demonic forces that had displaced Yahweh's truth and glory in their eyes. It started with Solomon, but reached its zenith of destruction through Jeroboam his successor.

If you remember, Jeroboam, who replaced Solomon, was extremely insecure about his new post as Israel's third king. He knew he was not of noble birth and really should not have been considered for kingship. Yet, Jehovah saw fit to install him, which He did by the hand of a prophet. After surveying the situation, Jeroboam imagined unreal threats to his kingdom. Terrified that he would lose his position if Judah continued to serve the very God who put him in power in the first place, he concocted a deadly solution. The account of the story in 1 Kings says his emotional insecurity drove him to rebel against the Lord and hand the kingdom over which Yahweh had caused him to reign, to devils. His defection, entirely spiritual, was nonetheless deadly. Today we would call it a new religious movement. Whatever the name, Jeroboam rewarded God's favor by plunging His treasured nation of Israel into a darkness from which they would never fully recover. In panic and selfishness, he created his own religious system, taking the country right out of Jehovah's hands and dominion and delivering it to the very gods (and demons) the Lord had rescued Israel from in the beginning. Jeremiah 2:11 calls it changing one's god.

Picking up from Solomon's defection, Jeroboam expelled the Levitical priests from the Lord's temple and put in their place those he chose out of his own heart. He installed all who showed an interest in the job, thus shifting the order of priestly progression from its Aaronic dynasty to commoners. He further changed Israel's holy days celebrations from what Moses by God ordained, to his own. The tragedy of his treason is seen in 2 Chronicles 11:14–15. Instead of ministering to and by the Holy Spirit that preserved and sanctified them, the new demonic priests now taught and promoted worship of devils. Read the account yourself to learn how the world of the prophets under Jeroboam was much like the world of today. Repeating cycles of perversion and heathenism masked as New Age revelation solidify the need for the prophet more than anything else.

False teaching, perverted truth, humanism, and worldliness all crowd out (and drown) the consciousness of the 21st century church. Mirroring Jeroboam's era, wide-scale classes publicize globally the ancient gods, goddesses, religions, and sorcery that historically have destroyed every nation that worshipped them. The modern media, financed by the antichrist spirit in the world, crams those very Eastern religions down our throats, as they proselytize for darkness.

Believe Not Every Spirit

Meanwhile, humanism scorns any hint of spirituality tied to Jesus Christ or the living God. Taken together, these signs incite powerful divine intervention and cry out for an equally powerful prophetic treatment. As you may well see from our Jeroboam discussion, the same devils and sorceries are being proliferated today under the guise of spiritual enlightenment, personal empowerment, and independence from religion and the Creator. Many people, unlearned in the word of the Lord, are seduced into thinking they are finding a better, easier way to God and/or redemption through these devious traps. Really they are being duped into believing they do not need Him because as masters of their own destinies or fates, they create their own heaven and hell. These souls fall prey to the most fiendish of all seductions, the *word* spiritualism; lumping all invisible and intangible encounters into one. Being enticed by metaphysical knowledge and psychic enlightenment, they drop their guards and are sucked into serving sin and death. What's more, many of those drawn down the yellow brick road to see the Wizard of Oz are Christians, at least they claim to be. Such saints, in love with the idea of spirituality, overlook the reality that not every spirit is of God (1 John 4:1). Poor discernment and still poorer Bible education makes them unable to tell whether something spiritual is of Creator God or not. But,

Jesus gave us a clue and it is that clue that prophets decipher for us, as seen in John 6:45. They decry the blurring of the lines separating godly from ungodly spiritualism. The prophet reiterates Christ's words in the above verse reminding us today that it is still all about the Lord Jesus Christ. One thing occultists hate and shudder at is the name of Jesus. That is why Christ distilled the whole of the redemptive strategy down to Himself and faith in His name.

An Antichrist Spirit Fuels Demonic Flames

Occultism's insidious renowned elevation in society's mind promotes sin and demonism blatantly through the most coveted icons of our culture. The ghastly and the ghostly have united to clutter the landscape of the invisible world with horrific powers with which mortal humans are not equipped to contend. Ungodly use of the supernatural and perversion of true spiritual power together demonstrates for us God's need for official prophets. The enormous spiritual enablement the Creator instilled in them drives back the hellish onslaught brewing to take hold of the modern world like never before.

To show these statements are not mere panic cried to defend religion or the church, ask yourself how much of what you encounter in your daily life smacks of demons, witchcraft, sorcery, and mysticism. Public school academic curriculums are flooded with them; the truth of the gospel in contrast denied equal exposure. Media ad campaigns and programming all force ancient religions and pagan rituals on you and your children. The very after-school and Saturday morning cartoons on television we all once trusted are now agents of this crude and cruel New Age agenda of occultism. And let us not forget the Internet and the technology world. One day go surf the web and see how often the names and teachings of ancient paganism are flaunted. Then you will know how drastic the situation is. The devilish campaign has been so relentless that it overwhelms many people and numbs Christians. Unaccustomed to such exposure to sin, they are so spellbound that they are at a loss for what to do, or wonder if anything need be done at all.

Truthfully, many people sense something is drastically wrong with all this, but without *pneuma* (spiritual) education and training to enlighten their academics, they just can't seem to figure out what. Again, here is where we need God's true prophets to shed light on the devices of darkness and instruct His people on true and false spirituality.

Why Prophetics?

The prophetic is the only prime choice because the Lord prepared it to stem the tide of demonism stalking our generation. What makes this so is the revelatory teachings of 1 Corinthians 14:32; Ezekiel 13:1–3; and Nehemiah 9:30. Together, these passages unmask a largely discounted reality concerning the prophet's makeup. The distinction sets the official prophet above the *prophesier.* It is the spirit within the prophet, not just the Holy Spirit, but the unique prophet's spirit alluded to earlier. The prophet's spirit makes the prophet a prophet, whether or not he or she becomes born again. The Holy Spirit in a person furthers the distinction by establishing whether or not the prophet uses his or her spirit for the kingdom of God under the dominion of Jesus Christ. Otherwise, the capacity to receive prophetic revelations and the ability to prophesy are generic to the prophet's natural birth. See the ministry of Balaam in Numbers 23–31. He was not under Israel's covenant and yet was used by God to see with his spiritual eyes what God planned for the nation he was paid to curse. The prophet says that his eyes were finally now wide open. That means that it was in this instant that the prophet came in contact with His Maker and the visions he saw he knew were real for the first time.

The differences between the two spheres of operations, saved and unsaved, can be narrowed down to three definite things: spiritual authority, divine license, and enforcement power. If a prophet converts to Jesus Christ, his or her gifts are sanctified and inspired by the entirely new impulses and objectives of God's Holy Spirit. Now, because of the officer's love for the Lord, operating these revelatory gifts serve a higher purpose and targets a quality of life that exceeds the temporal and material, going all the way to the eternal.

Quick Study Chart
Spiritual Equipment for Prophetic Service

The prophet's work after the New Birth in Jesus Christ brings hearers and learners alive due to their:

1. Love for God.
2. Commitment to holiness.
3. Righteous zeal.
4. Apprehension of divine truth.
5. Acceptance of humanity's sin condition.
6. Realization of the residual sin in the flesh of all believers.
7. Understanding the church's needs to mature in God.
8. Recognition that all mankind must repent and be saved.
9. Allegiance to God.
10. Determination to uphold God's truth on earth.
11. Fearless rebuke of God's people to warn them of impending danger.
12. Giving God's judgment on sin.
13. Surrender to a total loss of independence and identity in Christ.
14. Compliance with God's wishes, obedience, submission, or surrender.
15. Seeking and receiving proper God approved training.
16. Nurture and training of the flock of God.
17. Peculiar human insight for prophetic service.
18. Strength and conviction in things of God.

19. Defensiveness about Christ and His gospels.

20. Protection of God's kingdom and possessions.

21. Zealous safeguarding of God's sheep.

22. Reverence for God's sovereignty.

23. Righteous respect for God's judgments.

24. Disregard of worldliness in devotion to God.

25. Contempt for worldliness in the Body of Christ.

26. Constant longing for their heavenly home.

27. Aching for the redemption of God's lost sheep.

28. Certainty of God's final judgment on man and earth.

29. Eagerness to see the end of this age.

30. Need for God's continuous fellowship.

31. Strong sense of duty.

32. Regard for the gravity of official ministry service.

33. Knowledge of the scope of responsibility of prophetic office.

34. Knowledge of the full impact of the office's demands and influence on self and the world.

35. Comprehension of the outcome of prophetic work.

36. Relentless hunger for God's presence.

These all sanctify and empower by the *chrio* anointing the basic traits and the character of all prophets irrespective of their salvation in Jesus Christ.

Quick Study Chart
What Makes Prophets Prophets?

Heightened by the salvation process, these are called the Natives of the Prophet's Makeup. They are:

1. **Propensity for visions and dreams**—Dreams of a predictive, revelatory, and highly insightful nature.

2. **Sensitivity to spiritual things**—Ability to pierce the spheres of the flesh and spirit, the visible and invisible layers of cre-

ation, to perceive God's truth in action.

3. **Comprehension of prophetic matters**—Grasping the apparently superficial to identify and isolate its divine, supernatural, and apocalyptic roots and/or elements.

4. **Apprehension of role and place of prophecy**—Giving credence to the subtle yet lofty position and imposition of prophecy upon human life and earthly existence.

5. **Awareness of God,** most specifically Jesus, as prophecy— Understanding that there is a Creator, and that being true, accepting that what happens in the now is the direct result of what He has ordained and inscribed on His handiwork from eternity.

6. **Capacity for revelation discovery**—The ability to pull back the veils of humanism and secularism to uncover the hallowed, holy truths of the Almighty in a given situation.

7. **Peculiar interpretative skills**—Seeing things at face value while instinctively applying the probe of the Creator's truth to their meanings.

8. **Extraordinary wisdom and human insight**—Knowing that the wisdom from above, as James' epistle says, is first pure, then peaceable, and easy to entreat. As such, it is as the only answer to the woes and troubles of the world.

9. **Great sense of practical application**—Not being a hearer of the word of God, but a resolute doer of its work, resolving life's thorny issues with heaven's eternal remedies.

10. **Heightened spiritual discernment**—Recognizing that what is seen with the human eyes and discerned by human senses is merely the tip of the iceberg beneath which the truth lies as a deeply embedded reality that must be weighed against God's creation laws as officiated by His protocratic government.

11. **Inordinate grasp of scripture**—Regardless of the sacred writings prescribed to initially, it is to accept that to serve one's god apart from that written as the will, programs, and conditions of that service is futile. Plainly, serving the Living Lord is vain without due regard given to the written word of God.

12. **Deep hunger for the knowledge of God**—Exemplifying the need for the Lord as the God of one's ministry calling above the need for ministerial expression and fame.

13. **Potential for inspired utterance**—Inexplicably speaking forth truths, wisdom, and maxims that can only spring from a higher source, because they show themselves to be obviously relevant, timely, and accurate to the situations that inspire them.

14. **Remarkable accuracy of divine communication**—A deep-rooted sense of important Creator truths, an unbiased and objective representation of the things of the spirit realm and of God.

15. **Strong literary skill**—An uncanny knack for writing what is discerned from the Spirit of God whether or not it is understood or seen as relevant at the time of its writing.

16. **Impressive elocution and oration ability**—The ability to fearlessly say what must be said on behalf of the Lord, clearly, concisely, and persuasively without personal fillers, opinions, or bias whether the communication is spiritual or practical in origin. This is so despite its evidential or implied power to alter the status quo.

17. **Unusual judicial aptitude**—The peculiar and rare ability to discern the difference between right and wrong on the basis of what Creator God ordained, sanctioned, shunned, and rejected; instinctively knowing how and why the former is more excellent than the latter.

18. **Notable organization ability**—Apprehension of the reality that God is order, and to rightly represent Him and portray His high by intangible aptitudes one must be organized and prone to orderliness.

19. **Outstanding leadership ability**—Comprehending the ministry as a position of trust and leadership where sound principles and practices of getting the will of the Lord into followers and then performed by them is achieved.

20. **Influential government ability**—The wisdom to enact, legislate, and regulate the conduct, behavior, and pursuits of the benefited groups without sacrificing the Lord's best interests.

If you are going to be a church prophet, or a prophet of any type for the Lord Jesus Christ, you should be naturally exhibiting the twenty traits described above. That is, they should not have to be instilled in you, but rather refined through your prophetic education and service.

Why do you think the first thirty-six points and the last twenty points given are important to a prophet's ministry? When you consider your answers, review the lists again, and think about the problems or issues they address. Consider how the listed traits and characteristics translate to prophetic action that begets God's solutions. If you can see the practicality of the two, you are well on your way to understanding the prophetic and the ministry of the official prophet.

Are Prophets Really for Today?

Prophets are as much for today as ever. As long as God, the devil, and man all stay the same, the need for the prophet continues. Revelation 11 says they will continue until the end of this age. These three and the world are all interrelated and prophets and the prophetic law are how each one contacts and conveys information to and through one another.

It does not matter how modern we appear; closer scrutiny shows we have not progressed that far after all. We have noticed how technology names its work after the same demons the Lord has fought with since antiquity. When you purchase many computer programs, not to mention computer games, you are met with the names of ancient demons in the guise of their mythological images. Beyond this, the Internet floods us with ungodly figures and practices reviving them for a new round of age-old wizardry. In fact, the word wizard appears in nearly every computer program as if to compel us to embrace them in our society. For these reasons, God emphatically still needs prophets, especially since they balance the effects of psychics presently dominating their place on the supernatural front.

What Is a Prophet?

A prophet is a divine messenger of God (or any god). He or she is an official spokesperson for the deity served on earth. A prophet invokes the will, destiny, plans, and powers of God to manifest the spiritual and the supernatural in our world. Although prophets do this mainly by speaking, sometime they resort to drama, theatrics, song, or other demonstrative modes to depict the word of the Lord.

According to *Strong's Concordance,* the Greek word for prophet is *prophetes,* the word most accepted by the New Testament church. However, in concept it falls short of the ancient origins of the prophetic in its usage and applications because the Greeks saw the prophetic predominantly in oracular contexts. By the time they controlled the world, religious and therefore spiritual extremes were being pushed to the background. Therefore, they stressed mostly the prophesying rather than the performing and provoking work of the ministry. Most of the definitions we use today to explain the prophetic come from their limiting the office and its officers to this narrow field of revelatory activity.

The Hebrews on the other hand had a fuller connotation of the prophetic as conveyed in their meanings of the word. Their term shows an expansive understanding of the mantle in all its contexts. Their word is *nabi*. Unlike the Greek perception of the prophetic, the Hebrews, who derived their use of the minister from the ancients who preceded them, saw the prophet as much more than a simple *predictor*. For them, the ministry had a power-wielding influence that affected destiny and dramatically impacted the world around them. The *nabi* can be traced throughout history, its functions being documented as far back as man, religion, and God are recorded, after the Edenic transgression. It is these ancient models that the Israelites drew from to operate their prophetic ministry under Jehovah God.

The Distinctive of the *Nabi*

The *nabi* is expressly accepted as a divine agent of the supernatural world. The messenger's power is inherent in the spirit and flesh. The *nabi*, not unlike the *prophetes*, is spokesperson for a deity and so much more. This officer is also a teacher, predictor, and visionary who interprets dreams and visions, peers into the supernatural, and compels its invisible powers to perform and manifest themselves in the now. The *nabi* actuates spiritual powers to set in motion the events that take place in our world. See Daniel 1–4; Zechariah 3; and Amos 3:7. All these actions are in addition to the prophecies many of our churches today are accustomed to receiving from modern prophets.

Both the *prophetes* and the *nabi* include in their definitions, "one who stands in the *restricted* office of the prophet." That means one cannot arbitrarily decide to become a prophet no matter how much he or she mimics the mantle's operations. However, *nabi*'s meaning adds noteworthy dimensions that better insight us on the ubiquitous range of the prophet's power and authority. Its meaning includes, from ancient texts, "one who invokes the gods." Hence, when Yahweh told Moses his mouth would be as God to Aaron, and Aaron's would function as Moses' prophet—mouthpiece—to the people, both men fully perceived what He meant. See Exodus 4:15–16.

What all this says to us is that if the prophet, local church or not, is without a deity who vows to perform their words, the title of prophet is vain. That is how prophets get done what they do. The ancients understood this about the prophet sufficiently enough to include in their definition of the officer, the power to *invoke, summon, and marshal the powers and resources of the gods.* In our case, that would be the God of gods. The prophet or other authorized priest does so by invoking the name of the god.

Based on this, we, as Christians who are the New Creation priesthood of the Lord Jesus Christ, invoke His omnipotent power and authority by using His name and doing all we do in His name. John 14:14 and Colossians 3:17.

How Does One Become a Prophet?

Strictly speaking, one cannot in the classic sense become a prophet. According to the scripture, primarily Jeremiah 1, people are born prophets from their mother's womb. God merely awakens the prophet spirit in everyone called to the ministry. He does this by summoning them through visions and dreams (Numbers 12:6). The idea that a person can just step into and occupy the *office of the prophet,* no matter how much the ministry is desired, is non-biblical. While it is popular to lead Christians to believe that if they want to prophesy or serve as a prophet, all they need to do is to want it badly enough, scripture says this cannot happen. Prophets must have the spirit for the office. They must be able to receive and interpret divine communications, convey them to those of their eras, and fortify their gifts with the license to enforce their words on the stubborn forces that would obstruct their manifestations.

Key Prophetic Distinctions

The confusion over what makes a prophet, over what signifies one as a vessel of prophecy, or prophesier, is understandable. When one is strictly guided by the definition of a prophet most commonly given, confusion cannot help engender confusion. If one defines the prophetic exclusively by giving the word of the Lord, then anyone who says, "Thus says the Lord," or "the Lord told me" may be a prophet. But when one takes into account the *prophetes-nabi* definitions, then other important factors must be taken into account. Such as, does the prophet invoke the gods, and is the necessary covenant that God ordinarily binds Himself to at work? Does the prophesier exhibit the signs and executions of an official? These two alone help you see that much is needed by the one who would declare himself or herself to be a prophet. The Quick Study Chart below gives a few more necessary points to consider when making the decision.

Quick Study Chart
Summary of Prophet and Prophesier Characteristics

The Vessel

The most common question of all is that of the difference between the prophetic vessel—the one who utters prophecy—and the one who stands in the official stead of the prophet.

- The difference is the same as that between the official evangelist and the one who witnesses Jesus or shares the message of the gospel.
- Prophetic vessels are confined to the Holy Spirit's manifestations as spelled out in 1 Corinthians 12:3–11, while the prophet is not.
- Prophets are considered by God to be *officers* of His kingdom. That means they are *commissioned* by God and *delegated authority* that transcends the mere verbalization of a message.
- The vessel of prophecy is largely confined to prophesying and then by spontaneous unction of the Holy Spirit.

The Office

The prophet as an officer in contrast to the vessel of prophecy is one who actually exercises all the functions and activities of the office with minimal divine restraint. They employ broad discretionary latitude.

- The immediate factor that sets one apart from the other is the presence of the prophet's spirit. We talk more about this later.
- The prophet's spirit empowers and enables the prophet as an officer upon God's release to move in and out of His supernatural realms and territories almost at will.
- The power and authority a prophet walks in and exercises are akin to that employed by the Lord's angels.
- Prophets have, based on the above, invocative, actuative, and demonstrative authority and power.
- Another major difference between the two is the prophet also has enforcement power with that authority to provoke the performance of their words in the earth. This is due in part to the supernatural contingent of angels assigned their ministry.

Mimicking the Prophet

Unfortunately, many people want to be prophets so badly that they intrude into the office's spheres with no capacity, aptitude, or resource for it. What happens in these cases is that they operate on their soul sense rather than their New Creation spirits. This makes them susceptible to divining devils looking to give voice to their wills and actions in the earth through the power of a born-again spirit. Unintentionally, these people become vessels of divination without knowing it. Since the deity performing their words is not the Lord Most High, such prophets become adept at divining from devils and thus operate more as a psychic than a prophet. Recall Balaam's words when he finally met the Almighty. His words were that now he sees with eyes wide open. All the while he was operating his prophetics, he did so by the power of whatever divine spirit happened to be in his vicinity. While Balaam did not know the difference before that time, he surely discovered the distinction once the real God put a word in His mouth.

Generally speaking, the only one who can really identify and articulate that something is wrong with such prophetics is another New Creation prophet. This is according to the tenor of 1 Corinthians 14:29. Others may sense that something is wrong, but they are often unable to detect or express where the problem lies. It takes another professional prophet who can tell precisely what or why a prophetic operation they witness is wrong, and then many of them can only do so with sound reputable prophetic training and education.

If I'm Not a Prophet,
Do I Still Need to Learn About Prophetics?

The answer to the question is emphatically yes! Everyone who is saved should know about the prophetic because that is how the church came into existence. The Creator spoke about His plans to have a family, a people, and a nation, for Himself long before any of it came into being. Those spoken words acted on creation every day until the vision of God's heart came to be. That vision spoken by the Lord Himself and His prophets is what caused the church to be born. Hebrews 1:1–2 transmits this truth.

Being born as a direct result of the word of the Lord is what makes the church prophetic. God's auto-verbal acts and their processes are what the Creator calls prophetic. Auto-verbal means in this case, that which is set in motion by a spoken word, set to act by an embedded sign. When God is eternal, and thus outside of time, speaks to His world in time, that by definition is prophecy. That speaking is what the Father terms prophetic because the message originates outside of the world's time zones (from eternity) and finds its chronology in humanity. Its events are encoded in creation's calendars that reflect God's scheduled myriad of earthly events. This is the means by which prophecy is set in motion in its appointed times and seasons. Review Solomon's words in Proverbs 3:1–11 for biblical amplification.

Prophecy is set in time by way of the human medium who utters it. That medium may be a prophet, a prophetic vessel, a prayer warrior, intercessor, psalmist, or seer. While sometimes angels do this, prophecy still has to be empowered on earth through the utterance of the human voice. Prophet's doing so activates their word's implantation in the life or sphere of life of the hearer. Here is what God means by Isaiah 41:4 regarding the generations.

Why Do We Need Prophets When We Have the Holy Spirit?

Over the years, a misunderstanding of the scope of prophetic work has led many shortsighted Bible teachers to declare that the dwelling of the Holy Spirit in a life eliminates the need for the prophet, the official prophet that is. Many have contended that the presence of the Holy Spirit within makes everyone who is saved his or her own prophet. Others add that the operation of the gifts of God as specified in 1 Corinthians 12:3–11 more than establishes the church's independence of the prophet, yet they are emphatically named in Ephesians 4:11 and 1 Corinthians 12:28–29.

Practically speaking, even though we have the Holy Spirit, people often cannot hear God clearly enough or frequently enough for themselves. Moreover, those that do hear God, frequently find they misunderstand what the Lord really means or is actually saying. Ordinarily His language is different from our own because His word and will are not obliged to our cultures or their morays. This is because God is Spirit and we are flesh. God as spirit means He is invisible. Since we cannot see Him, He must speak to us through tangible means. His nature being Spirit says that when He does speak, without concrete means of substantiating His sounds and their meanings, people invariably misunderstand what the Lord is saying. Think about the time that Jesus spoke to His

Father and God answered Him in John 12:28–29. Some people heard the sound as words; others heard it as thunder. That is how it is today. Other examples may be gotten from reading John 8:41–43 and Hebrews 12:19–20.

In the John reference, Jesus spoke in their own language and yet the content of what He said completely escaped their understanding. In the Hebrews reference, the strictness of the Lord's word on the hearers was more than they could bear. The rigidity of God's word would not bend for what they perceived as unjust punishment on an animal too ignorant to stay out of harm's way. To those who looked on, the animal's death on account of infringing upon the Lord's holiness was nothing but Jehovah slaying an innocent victim. That it would die without knowing why, was too harsh for the people to accept, so they begged Moses not to make them hear the Lord firsthand anymore. These examples point out the reasons why the prophet is needed in the local church, and how those who inquire of God should do so through them. People lack God's lofty righteousness which Psalm 71:19 says is very high. Except someone of understanding and wisdom brings it down, there is no way for people to grasp or regard it.

Just think about how differently you hear and understand information from how the Lord does. I once said to a group of people that we can take years or decades to comprehend one complete thought from God. He can start in January and probably have to wait a year or more for us to understand what He said and what He meant. Take the following example as a case in point. In January we pray and hear the Lord say "go." Our immediate response is to figure out what He meant. Did He mean go to the store, to the missions, to the church? What? After struggling on our own for a while, we finally settle down to get the rest of the message.

Remember now, several weeks may have gone by. The next word comes: "Go to the place." While we have more information to go on, there is still a final piece missing. Why won't the Lord just say what He means and get it over with, you think? Why does He put you through the games? Again, a few weeks of personal probing and then you decide you can go back to the subject with the Lord again.

At last He says it, and gets the entire sentence out: "Go to the church on the corner." You are stunned. The church on the corner, you ask. What church? Now you are playing games because you know that there is only one church on the corner and it is the little storefront one you would not be caught dead in. God knows your heart, you think. He could not possibly ask you to sink down to that level. Oh, you must have mistaken what He said. You inwardly regret pressing the point and wish you had not heard what He said. Since no one else heard Him but you, you begin the most dangerous of all prophetic games. You begin to twist the word you heard to cause it to say something you can live with and . . . who is to know the truth anyway, you rationalize. Three months have gone by and you pressed the Lord into an answer and now you do not like it. Silently, you determine not to do it and put the entire matter behind you. What's next? Judgment.

God must send you through an assortment of excruciating—pride breaking—lessons for you to obey Him. He knew all along that you would react this way, but now that it is out in the open, He is forced to correct this flaw in your character and end your presumptive disobedience. It gets hard and after years, what should have been a twenty-second inquiry and response has turned into a terrible test of wills, yours against the Lord's. Years go by, you miss the blessing He had buried for you in that little no name, unattractive church, but nonetheless, the stronghold over your soul must be broken, and so it goes. Could the prophet have made a difference?

Although you may not have listened to the prophet, the matter could have been greatly expedited by your hearing the entire command the first time. Perhaps you would have shaved three to six months off the search time and maybe been persuaded to obey in time enough to reap the re-

ward of obedience the Lord had for you in the place you secretly de-
spised. Prophets grasp God's thoughts and intents quicker than others
do. They are attuned to His way of communicating because that is how
He constructed them and over the years their training conditioned them.
Let's look at some of the differences between how the Lord thinks and
speaks and how we do. Review the Quick Study Chart below for a deeper
appreciation of the difference.

Quick Study Chart
God's Thoughts Through Prophets

*If you are a school, class, or prophetic study group, spend time discussing the
statements here and explaining how they are important to what the Lord
needs from the prophets in general, and those He sets in the church.*

The prophet learns early that:

- God thinks in whole thoughts. We think in fragments.
- He says what He means in one statement. We often find it
  difficult to digest His statements all at once. It takes in comparison, strings of statements to make our point.
- We understand the Lord and His style of communication bit
  by bit.
- God thinks and operates omni-creationally. We are primarily
  limited to His earthly.
- God approaches His handling of the earth from heaven down.
  We, on the other hand, process what He does from the earth
  up.

Prophets are trained to help people grasp what God is thinking, saying,
and willing for their lives from God's perspective. Even with the Holy
Spirit within us, our busy lives, difficulties, and crises can all cause us to
misunderstand God at different times. It is then that we need God's proph-

ets to inject His objectivity into our dilemmas. Prophets compel us to face the truth about ourselves, our motives, and our personal agendas. They make us, whether we admit it publicly or not, recognize when we are imposing our will on God to have our way. They make it hard for us to explain away our manipulations under a religious veneer.

Theological Doctrine Needs Wisdom's Prudence

As long as theology and doctrine separate themselves from human necessity and life application, such statements make as much sense as any other does. Notwithstanding, that is not the case with God. His word and His requirements are not merely intellectual in object, although they are quite intelligent. God is pursuing a definite aim in our lives with His word: that of His work, holiness, righteousness, and eternal qualification of the redeemed for everlasting life. Therefore, for every principle, precept, function, and activity detailed in the Bible, there is a corresponding human condition, attitude, conduct, or belief that inspired it. Prophets easily grasp this truth which substantiates their calling and defines their jobs. That is how they can tell you why the Lord called them and empowers their mantles. Prophetics are God's way of getting His word into society, His will to work in its cultures. Depending upon their generations and the eras in which their words are assigned, prophecies are ignited by the mouths of God's prophets. Their ministries actuate and craft the prophetic words God implanted in creation for their times. See 2 Chronicles 36:22–23.

The pattern goes back to eternity, as we have shown that prophetics are how God brought His Son Jesus into the planet. It began with the word to Zechariah announcing the birth of John the Baptist and six months later repeated itself with Mary, who was visited by the angel Gabriel. Both events were occasioned by the Lords use of prophecy.

Centuries of prophetic words brought the Savior into the earth. His conception was the culmination of God's constant stream of encoded, inflexible prophecies from the mouths of His servants. Their words shaped the events and birthed the people who eventually brought Jesus to planet earth.

Today, the church scarcely dares to think that Jesus arrived in the planet by the invisible vehicle of continuous prophecy spoken by the prophets over thousands of years. Yet to respect and have faith in prophecy, you are going to need to begin to think of prophecy as more than sounds from highly spiritual people. You are going to have to see with your spiritual eyes the teams of angels and the hosts of supernatural resources that go into action at the moment the words "thus says the Lord" are declared.

At the beginning of the prophetic process, it seems the words are not going to happen, but if the messenger is a true prophet of God with the prophet's spirit, then rest assured the word will come to pass. That is, in prophetic language, they will manifest their physical states in our world over time. What occurs behind the scenes is the early stages of prophecy—the manifestation development (PM development). The prophet's words initially act as blue prints, gathering resources, and agency activators that set the stage for the gestating process which births the message's physical form. An elaborate network of episodes and procedures go into action when a genuine prophetic word leaves God's mouth. Isaiah 55:11 gives some insight into the chain reactions the Lord's word ignites to give earthly life to His prophecies.

Situations and Circumstances That Bring Us God's Prophets

When the season for something the Lord has inscribed upon the tablets of creation arrives, think back to His engraving the Ten Commandments on stone. It is at these times that God sends us another prophet or prophetic word. His aim is to transmit to us by supernatural means to get His words and will to us to kindle our faith enough to cooperate with His ordained circumstances. Sometimes they introduce what God is doing or going to do. Other times they confirm what He has been telling us all along. Here is another reason why we need prophets. To be sure we have heard from God, He sends us prophets to reiterate what He has been saying in our spirits. This is especially true when the matter is important to destiny and the divine will of our Lord. It does not matter if the word is positive or negative in our eyes. It is from the Lord and that makes it, if not good to us, then good for us.

Hidden Dangers in Self Prophecy

Since many people do not like to confront or hear the truth, many of them avoid it any way they can. This character trait means that with or without the Holy Spirit, they will certainly not be inclined to prophesy truth to themselves. When the inquiry to God is regarding a dire matter or something they really feel they must have, the principle of Ezekiel 14:14 will most likely kick in. In urgent times or in moments of great need or desire, the conflict of interest becomes so great that their customary sound discernment can fail. If such people are honest with themselves and the Lord, they will admit their vulnerable state and seek God's answer from credible prophets. If their church has a properly functioning house prophet institution, they can turn to such a group for quality guidance and accurate prophecy. That is why God needs prophets overall, and in His church particularly.

Prophets are special when they are yielded to God because they can take God's truth for themselves, and no matter how hard it is, they find it easy to administer that truth to others. Truly the law of "first partaker" is well ingrained in them prior to public service. The practice is compelled upon the prophet by the Lord to assure their balanced objective ministers to Him.

Why Does God Continue His Prophetic Institution

Because we will spend eternity with the Most High God, we must learn all we can about how He does things in His world. While the need for prophecy may be altered in the future, its functional concepts go on, based on the rewards the Lord promised to those of the church who endure to the end. When you think about the Pergamos church (Revelation 2:17) for instance, the eternal stone promised the overcome is symbolic of a revelation instrument. It equates to the Old Testament Urim and Thummim of the Levitical priesthood. In other words, that stone with the new name of the bearer etched in it designates who the bearer is in Christ's New Kingdom, how they are to serve, and how they receive their instruction and insights from the Lord. Remember, we said earlier that prophecy is the communications media of the spirit world? It is how its citizens pass on thoughts, activities, plans, and the will of God to one another, between themselves, and to us. God's eternal protocol having been fixed in eternity binds the earth to the same parameters for information exchanges between the two worlds.

Getting Back to Our Eternal Roots

The people of this world have to return to their Creator-endowed spiritual roots of communicating. Spiritual communication relies on more than the six senses. When one realizes that five of the six senses depend on the flesh and the sixth one is confined to the soul realm, it is easy to see how and why mankind was shut out of spiritual knowledge. It is also understood why the extent of ethereal information we receive is limited to the *psuche* (psychic) realm of human existence. What is lacking in our reconnection to the Creator is a medium of *pneuma* (spirit) communication. Transmissions from the Spirit of God to the spirit of man are outside the customary means imposed on us for receiving supernatural knowledge. This helps explain how witchcraft, sorcery, and demonology in general are, according to God, mere works of the flesh. See Galatians 5:19. Since six is the number of man, and the five senses serve the body, then what mortals deem as supernatural is still light years away from the Creator. Thus six and the flesh have more to do with the soul realm than the spirit and so humans must access another sphere to interact with God. The answer comes from Isaiah 26:9 where the Lord through His prophet identifies the difference between the activities of the soul and the spirit. The spirit is how one seeks and worships the Lord. Jesus confirms it in John 4:23–24. When it comes to the occult, since they are all products of the soul realm and the earth, this makes them works of the flesh. Furthermore, it gives us insight as to how they came to be designated as fleshly works, although they masquerade as spirituality. You only need to reread Revelation 12:12–13 to see the picture. As much as the devil's clan wants you to believe that he is the height of spiritual power, in reality that is what he lost when he was cast out of heaven. All he and his devils were left with was earthly power, such as that conferred on Adam when he lost in the Eden's contest. Here is what the Lord Jesus meant when He said He saw Satan fall as lightning from heaven (Luke 10:18). What he fell from was his celestial station into the spheres of the terrestrial, and terrestrial means earthly, worldly, and physical. To match Isaiah's description of true God contact, one must draw on their spirit. Then they can be assured of His being the spiritual connection they make by becoming born again. Otherwise, all supernatural interactions are soulish and fleshly.

Human's Seventh Sense

The New Testament on the other hand, gave us a better analogy. It talks about the hidden man of the heart, the spirit man, and mentions the abolition of the wall of partition between them that the Savior accomplished for us on the cross. What is meant by this is that the divider between the soul and spirit (Hebrews 4:12) that veiled the latter from the former was disintegrated by the work of the cross. Christ's doing so allows something to happen that had not been possible since Adam's fall. That is the communication and information exchange between the two intangible parts of humanity's makeup. Because of the work the Lord did on the cross, the spirit can now communicate to the soul and vice versa.

Pure streams are possible, whereas before Christ, they were not.

The name for the spirit's role in the supernatural affairs of the human life is "seventh sense." It speaks to spiritual knowledge and intelligence. What makes this true is that seven is the number of the spirit—God's spirit world, while six is the number of man and Satan. See Revelation 3:18 and 1:4; 4:5; 5:6. These all show the difference between the sixth (souls) sense and seventh (New Creation) spirits and how they relate to the supernatural faculties of humans. Prophets are obliged to be cognizant of this truth if they are to discern when an utterance originates from the Lord God or one of His fallen creatures. This includes the dark side of the human heart as Ezekiel 13:1–3 shares.

What makes all this relevant to the prophet is the reason they are important to society first and to the church second. The prophet's importance to the world stems from the human inability to hear from and comprehend the communications of the spirit realm. A barrier separates the soul from the spirit in most of humanity, and God compensated for it by endowing a select class of people with the ability to pierce the veil that blinds us to His world and permit their access to its information streams. Essentially, this is why we need prophets. In the church their value may not appear so evident until one considers how biased each of us is to our own views, feelings, desires, and pursuits. Hence the institution of the prophetic confers objectivity on the members of the body so they get God's unbiased position on their circumstances and matters. Through His reliable prophets, the Lord impels truthful responses to our inquiries regardless of what we feel or desire, and remember that desire is seated in the soul realm. The New Creation spirit is truth and the soul is you. Therefore, when the two are actively communicating and exchanging information, the answers we receive from the Lord are accurate. Ethical prophets force us to hear the word of the Lord on a matter, and if we are honest, we know and accept what we have heard to be from God. They bring you to Christ (John 6:44–45), who is the Spirit of prophecy.

Chapter 3

HISTORY OF
THE PROPHETIC

Where Most Prophetic Genre Originates

The most comprehensive background existing today that elucidates us on the office and institution of the prophet, along with its functions, come from the ancient Mari texts discovered in the early 19th century largely by Andre Perot. Mari, or El Hariri as it is known today, was in the vicinity of modern Syrian Iraq. In Bible times, it was an ancient city of Mesopotamia settled on the middle section of the Euphrates River. The Maris were a mountainous people under the control of primitive Babylon until their demise. Their most significant king was Hammurabi. Until destroyed for their superiority and independence, they were known for extraordinary spirituality and supernatural advancement. Today we call it New Age occultism. Mari is credited with one of the most extensive and sophisticated systems of prophetics ever traced.

Prophets in their land served many functions throughout society and were as influential as royalty, nobility, or the priesthood. Mari's prophetic institution assigned prophets to their palace, their civil offices, and in their sanctuaries or temples.

Mari History

In the Bible, the Mari may be recognized as the descendants of the ancient Amorites whose rule and inheritance the Lord swore to give to the seed of Abraham (Genesis 15:16–21). The Amorites came from the Canaanites who originally inhabited Palestine. Their name means "a sayer," an inscription that points to their extraordinary prophetic ability, as perverse as it was. By the time Israel fulfilled God's word, the Mari system had intricately merged with the Canaanite orders and practices of the supernatural. See 1 Kings 21:26 and 2 Kings 21:11. Ezra 9:1 says that by this time, the culture of this formidable enemy was well entrenched in Israel's consciousness. It is that institution reshaped and renamed that you see in today's occultic world. Go over the list of their occultic practices and notice their exact replication in our modern times.

- Astrology
- Necromancy
- Hydromancy
- Hepatomancy
- Fortune telling
- Palm reading
- Spiritism

We discuss these later under the subject of psychics.

Mari influences form the basis for what both the Christian church and secular occultists use in prophetic (or psychic as the case may be) ministry.

The Amorites equate to a spiritual nemesis the Lord has dealt with since Nimrod, whose pagan religions settled in their line, although they were fathered by Canaan. The point is the Amorites are the subject of Bible discussion since the time the Lord cut covenant with Abraham in Genesis 15:16. It seems that at that time they were the ruling world power and somehow spiritually linked to the Lord's earthly center, then Jebus and today Jerusalem. Ezekiel 16 says that Jerusalem was founded by an Amorite and mothered by a Hittite. That is why it is viewed as having been Syria Palestinian. Ezekiel 43:7 says Jerusalem was always God's throne and footstool. Today its Amorite spirit would be situated in Palestine, since that is where their land was in 1830–1550 B.C., according to *Unger's Bible Dictionary.*

The Amorites were a perverse though highly evolved race of people. Their supernatural abilities were impressive and well documented over the years. When Babylon became a world power, much of its spiritual sophistication came from these people. Down through the years Amorite spirituality resurfaces under new names and renamed deities. Nonetheless, their works are well testified to, and over time abominable religious conduct became synonymous with them. Read 1 Kings 21:26 and 2 Kings 21:11. If you read also the seventh chapter of Revelation, Israel's lost tribe of Dan—by that time—says Judges 1:34–36 merged with the Amorites because they failed to defeat and expel them from their inheritance. Dan never returned to Yahweh wholeheartedly, says Judges 18:26–31. That means that all the years of their existence, Dan was an occult center where demons and witches took refuge and prospered, and it cost them their eternal position with God, according to Revelation 7.

The Mari/Amorite system of religion cycles itself because its spirit lives on in the planet and will until the end of time. Their name may be gone, but their fruit is still used by the spirits of darkness. They constitute a significant role in the spiritual principalities of God. We have named them His spiritual protocratics because they existed before the word was and continue to guard and govern the earth as it stands today. There is the Lord's kingdom of light protocratic and those of the kingdom of darkness.

Earth's Continued Need for Heavenly Assigned Spiritual Powers

Little has changed in the realm of mankind since time began in relation to spirituality. The earth still needs supernatural agents and their human representatives to spiritually inspire its conduct (Job 32:8; Isaiah 11:1–5; Ephesians 1:17). They mediate earth's transactions with God's spiritual citizenry. Sin, sickness, disease, error, lies, lewdness, and unbelief, as well as death and darkness are all standing reasons for the prophet's work in the world and in the local church.

The world's historical chronicles all cite primitive cultures' belief in an invisible force of powers backing the physical creation. It was accepted that they controlled all its activities and events. Exodus 23:23; 32:34; Joshua 5:13; Daniel 10:21; and Revelation 22:16 all show the truth of that belief. I have dubbed this force God's supernatural protocratics. As His spiritual powers of eternity, they see to the provisions He allocated to the earth. The apocalypse of Jesus Christ penned by the apostle John unveils them for us under the New Testament dispensation. In the Old Testament, many books did so, but none more poignantly than as the writings of the prophets Daniel and Zechariah. Collectively, all writings show us that what the ancient people believed was true according to the Creator. Angels were watching over them and taking care of their human matters.

Actually, it would make good sense on God's part to do so since He knew that humanity would be confined in their world to what their five senses could touch. God knew Adam's fall meant that much of what He had created would be unknown and inaccessible to them. So, He answered the problem with prophets acting on eternity's behalf and in Christ's stead on earth to compensate for humanity's lost spiritual roots. The Lord enabled prophets' invisible selves to lead their worlds to discover that they were not alone on earth. His aim was to get people to perceive that all earthly events were the direct result of the supernatural initiatives of His powerful invisible creatures.

To serve effectively as a prophet in this and the coming age of mankind, one must be educated in these truths, a requirement of the prophets of Samuel and Elijah's day accepted. One should be knowledgeable of the historic roots of the prophetic to justify its need in today's and future generations. To appreciate prophets' present worth, one must relate it to their original value to God and people. Doing so implants their need in the mind of the Lord's church. That need is endorsed by the apostle Paul's revelation of God's invisible principalities and powers, those spiritual protocrats we spoke of earlier. Their presence tell God's apostles and prophets, the two most powerful officers of the New Testament church according to 1 Corinthians 12:28–29 and Ephesians 4:11, that they are not alone. Not only are they part of an elaborate earthly regime, they are supported by complicated and infinitely more powerful heavenly authorities. Titus 3:1 says we are to obey them as well as those we see in the flesh. What are they? They were known of old as the seven *archons* of creation to the ancient world. You will learn from this section that they secretly prefigured the seven angels of the New Creation *ekklesia*.

The book of Enoch discusses eternity's supernatural *archons* in great detail, and until John's apocalypse they were scarcely uncovered in scripture—but they are there. Zechariah's prophecy mentions them almost casually as the "seven eyed priestly stone of the high priest Joshua." What embedded metaphors of the Lord Jesus and His church! Revelation 5:17 resurfaces those seven eyes, but this time they are on the seven horns of the Lamb and are defined as the seven spirits of God which are sent forth into all the earth. But, as antiquity's *archons*, how are we to know them? The answer is mostly by what they do. These are the powers that amazingly coincide with the seven churches of the Lord Jesus Christ discussed in scripture—those seven spirits the Revelation tells us eventually blanketed the earth, which ended up being divided into seven continents.

Seven is an important number in scripture, applied nearly five hundred times. In most of those times, seven is used in religious, prophetic, and apocalyptic contexts. That makes it quite important to the Lord in setting time, limiting events, and other significant Creator ordinances.

Beyond this is the obvious, that there are seven days per week and the seventh day being doubly important as the Sabbath. Now this is biblical genre we are talking about here, not occultic. God decreed the number as the unit of completion, thoroughness, and spiritual dominance. Among these is the most profound of all, those seven spirits before His throne. However, what they do or govern may make more sense to you. Here is a list of what those seven powers oversee as first eternity's seven *archons* and today the seven angels of the New Creation *ekklesia*. Their names and areas of effect are followed by a brief description. Bear in mind as you read them that no society or culture on earth exists without every one of them functioning, no matter what names they may be called by. I call them the seven spheres of creation over which God's spiritual protocrats rule.

Quick Study Chart
God's Seven Protocratic Spheres

- Worship and ritual
- Family and community
- Business and commerce
- Mammon: money and economy
- Government and administration
- Military warfare
- Education and communication

No matter where one goes on the planet, or in what society they sojourn, they will find that these seven spheres of human life prevail. Here is a brief explanation of each one.

    1. Worship and ritual—The worship and ritual system ordained by a deity. They are based on the character, functions, abilities, and authorities of the spirit worshipped, and coincide with the ways the deity or spiritual power was designed to access or employ God's supernatural resources. Unwritten protocols establish that worship and religious observance are the only ways for humans to access God's higher powers' resources. These are crafted and imposed upon the citizens of our world by the spirits that govern them or their territory. Under the New Creation church dispensation, the priest who met Abram after the slaughter of the five kings, Melchizedek, is the principalic officiate of this realm. It too is connected with Christ's church, as its eternal priestly order over which the Father God made Jesus High Priest. His *ekklesia*'s priesthood is derived from this lineage.

2. **Family and community**—To multiply, every culture has families and a multiplicity of families to create communities, tribes, nations, etc. The household culture that evolves from obedience to Genesis 1:28 make this a perpetual sphere in creation. Every institution born to man arose as a result of the family.

3. **Business and commerce**—Increased populations generate needs that different citizens gifts and talents must supply. These form the basis for an exchange system that over time establishes business and commerce. What one person makes translates to what another buys, because he or she sees it as valuable or essential. Buying and selling systems emerge as makers charge sellers something of value for their goods and services.

According to Proverbs 8–9, Lady Wisdom, a principality in herself, rules this sphere of human resources. Later, we see that it is, and was, Christ all along. In Him is hid all the treasures of wisdom and knowledge. Deuteronomy 8:18 says this sphere releases a specially endowed ability imparted by

God under covenantal circumstances. The prophet Isaiah wrote that it was the Lord that taught His people to profit (Isaiah 48:17).

4. **Mammon: Monetary Economy**—A thriving commercial system eventually develops a currency that turns into a monetary system. The places where money is stored are called banks, and their management of money in relation to the goods and services made constitute the sphere of finance. It is what Christ called mammon. When communities grow and accumulate wealth and riches through its exchanges, a spiritual principality manages that function that goes all the way back to eternity and Lucifer's kingdom, according to Ezekiel 28. The natural counterpart to this supernatural function, from Ezekiel 28, is found in Psalm 107:23.

5. **Government and administration**—Rules transformed into laws control citizen wrongdoing and curb destruction of the land and its best interests. Once drafted, the laws comprise the people's constitutional code of living. Laws successfully establishing order comprise government. Notice that the first thing the Lord did when He brought His new nation into existence was to issue a law for them. Judah, based on Psalm 60:7 and 108:8, is God's lawgiver. The New Creation church sprang, as did its founder, from the tribe of Judah.

6. **Military and warfare**—A government's power and authority, sure to be challenged and its laws tested, makes enforcement necessary. Preserving the government and protecting its community is done by a military—communal, civil, and national. These include a land's police and armed forces. When Joshua was to take over Moses' rulership, he was inaugurated on two levels. See Numbers 27:19 and Deuteronomy 31:14. After that, the Lord introduced Joshua to the spiri-

tual power that would see to his victories. Joshua 5:13–15 says a spiritual man appeared as captain of the Lord's armies. That host never left Israel, as 2 Kings 6:17 shows. Deborah, a military judge under Jehovah's hand, experienced them also. See Judges 5:20,23.

7. **Education and communication**—What makes a society profitable comes from its citizens being made productive. They must learn skills, talents, and trades to contribute to the wealth of the community and to afford what they need to buy to survive themselves. Communication addresses the basic need to transmit thoughts and understand others. A uniform way of transmitting thoughts, feelings, and ideas creates a communication system.

All the above seven are found in every society and are jointly administered by their respective heavenly and earthly principalic agents, and the prophets. It does not matter how crude, primitive, or sophisticated the system, these all prosper within a thriving civilization. Prophets are made aware of their principalities early in their training. God sees to it that they know and can recognize the spiritual forces that truly govern and control our world. Take as a case in point, the watcher over Nebuchadnezzar and his kingdom in the book of Daniel. Zechariah 3:1–9 gives an example of this in action, as does Ezekiel 9:1–11 and 2 Chronicles 20:20.

Functional Divisions of Prophetic Office

Based on the recognition of God's creation spheres, consistent with this premise, the prophet's office is divided into similar spheres that reflect these invisible powers, and differentiate prophetic personalities and anointings as assigned by the Lord. Interestingly, since they track with seven spheres of creation, you can by studying them identify a prophet's distinct prophetic concentration. Prophetic division benefits the particular area of prophetic treatment dispensed through the Lord's various prophetic mantles. No matter how versatile, prophets generally concentrate themselves into discrete areas of the human experience. Thus prophetic assignments footprint creation's spheres and are supported by scripture. For instance, take Daniel's ministry. It is easy to see that the sphere of prophetics his mantle concentrated on was *government*.

Other examples are Ezekiel and Isaiah, who seem to have served the sphere of the *ecclesiastical*. Amos fit the category of agriculture, or in our terms, the *laborer*. Moses' call centered on *monarchy*, while his brother Aaron's mantle settled on the *priestly*. Deborah and Joshua manifested their prophetics as *military* leaders. The prophetess Huldah appeared to concentrate on *education* with Elijah and Elisha, whose mantles doubled as *power* prophetics. Agabus and Silas both showed themselves as prophets called to *apostolic companionship,* while Gad, Iddo, and Shemaiah were *seer* prophets. Samuel emerges as a *shepherding* prophet, David's Nathan a *temple* prophet. Jeremiah illustrates a *reformation* prophet.

It is helpful to note this diversity of prophetic giftings to recognize where you fit in God's revelatory service or to identify the prophetic sphere of those prophets who serve you in God's kingdom. What follows outlines the typical distribution of prophetic work.

Contrary to what most believe, prophets do more than just walk around prophesying every day. They must, if they are to do their jobs, leave their prayer closets and serve the Lord's best interest by ministering to His people. Below are some of the things that go into prophetic work. As you can see, they broaden the traditional narrow stream of the ministry considerably.

Quick Study Chart
God's Use of Prophet's Faculties
· **Visions**—Open-sighted divine communications

- **Dreams**—Divine communications received while asleep
- **Symbols**—Translation of icons and emblems that represent something God wants to use in prophetic language
- **Parables**—Communication of prophecy using daily life imagery
- **Similitudes**—Divulging supernatural knowledge by way of comparisons and contrasts
- **Words of wisdom**—Conveying the prophetic insight and applied understanding for God's practicality in everyday affairs
- **Words of knowledge**—Declaring something God knows to another unable to be known or discovered by natural means
- **Prophecy, prediction and revelation**—Unveiling the Lord's hidden information and truths, regardless of the era, and foretelling them as prophecy
- **Divine decrees**—Actuating and turning the events of this world so they line up with the embedded commands and programs of the Lord
- **Declarations and commands**—Provoking the will and works of God to the extent of overriding the works of darkness and altering the normal course of life's events without prophetic intervention
- **Intercessory prayer**—Intervening with God and His spiritual activities to alter their occurrence in the world
- **Supernatural intervention**—Positioning oneself through prayer, service, sacrifice between impending catastrophe and its victim to reverse or restore the enemy's assault with the Lord Jesus' authority
- **Spiritual watch care**—Patrolling and stationing oneself in one's assigned prophetic ward to guard and prosper those in one's charge
- **Spiritual guardianship**—Encircling a territory either by divine

assignment or church position as the supernatural power force that stays the hands of judgment and/or obstructs demonic infiltration by exerting prophet's authority to enforce the will of the Lord on human situations

- **Praise war**—Conducting formal or informal spiritual worship sessions to facilitate the spiritual battles behind the scenes that one's prophetic guard is engaged in on behalf of those within the prophet's watch

Quick Study Chart
Spectrum of Prophet's Word

From what we have discussed so far, you can see that being a prophet is hard work. But that is not all. Here are a few more things the prophet must be occupied with that many of them do naturally, though only a few can explain why or how.

- **Tongues and interpretation**—Supernatural prayer in the spirit that transforms itself into the tongues of angels and sometimes the ancient tongues of old spiritual powers
- **Discerning spirits**—The ability to see physically or intuitively discern the presence of God's invisible creatures, angels, or demons
- **Psalms and poetics**—The activation of the aesthetic side of the prophet's mantle that resorts to songs, rhymes, and rhythmic sounds to release or give the word of the Lord
- **Seers**—Interaction with the mainly visual deliverer of messages from the Spirit of God
- **Dreamer of dreams**—Receiving or confirming the word of the Lord as revealed through dreams and night visions
- **Supernatural stratagems**—Meetings with God in special prophetic sessions (awake or asleep) to get His mind and plans on the tasks He is presently dispensing to His prophetic staff

- **Spiritual offerings, sacrifices and servitude**—Performing, confirming, and instructing others in God's true spiritual service requirements, their methods, value, and benefits
- **Spiritual warfare**—Joining by prayer, praise intercession God's invisible forces deployed to the earth to compel the fulfillment of His word, or invoke through prophetic power their actuation
- **Power sieges**—Setting up, through prayer vigils, relentless praise to create prophetic resistance and erect supernatural barriers around the enemy's camp; the aim is to halt his progress or frustrate his stratagems
- **Power confrontations**—Confronting sin, error, heresy, and perversion with the authority of the prophet's mantle and standing off with the works and forces of darkness to defend the church, faith, and flock of God
- **Discernment of heresy and heretical messengers**—Detecting and correcting erroneous teaching, trendy doctrine, or scripture dilution; marking and publicizing what is emphatically errant teaching as measured against the word of the Lord in scripture
- **Prophetic drama**—Portraying the word of the Lord in action, set to music or dance; depicting the invisible activities of eternity in public theatrics to demonstrate to worshippers what the Lord is doing behind the scenes

The Prophet's Mantle

One of the captivating things about the ministry is the mantle that an officer wears. It designates him or her as God's servant. Outward garments worn by servants reflected every ministry position in times past. They were important and no serious worker would start their tour of duty without wearing theirs. The attire they donned was meant to convey the essence of the worker's profession, sender, or principal.

In the case of many ancient officers, the sender was a deity and so invisible. The god's invisibility made it necessary for physical symbols to depict its power, authority, reputation, and image to followers. These had to be made to show the people their gods and identify his or her workers as members of the deity's staff. Call to mind on this subject the Lord's instructions to Moses about the priest's garments.

Thus, the servants of Baal in the Old Testament wore distinctive garb that reminded his worshippers of the god to whom they belonged. Headdresses worn were usually etched with an image: an animal, fish, or lightning bolt to symbolize the inherent presence and power residing in the deity's minister. With goddesses it was no different. Their servants too dressed in attire that represented them and their kingdoms and portrayed the power they possessed and wielded. For instance, Ishtar's priests often were transvestites and wore feminine clothing to imitate the goddess.

When the Lord God Jehovah established Himself as Israel's God, He took great pains to tell them how they would and would not look to the other nations. Likewise, His priests were admonished to adorn themselves exactly as He commanded with no variation whatsoever. No fertility emblems that imaged pagan gods were to be worn before Him. The people were not to look at the priest's attire and be inspired to resort to their pagan rituals and orgies. Again, the purpose was to not only depict Yahweh, Israel's God, but to also not misrepresent His image to His people and cause them to serve another deity in His place.

Today we would call such outfits uniforms of service, and they would be the equivalent of those worn by our civil, religious, and military workers.

Mantles Signified the Prophet

Throughout all history, the mantle signified the prophet. Every prophet dispatched by a deity wore select garments that brought to mind their stature and epitomized the nature of their messages as delivered to them from their gods. Elijah's hairy garment is a good example of this, as was John the Baptist, who inherited it. While we all know such outfits may not be needed under the New Testament era, their symbolic counterparts do apply. Otherwise, how else could John the Baptist have been recognized as the resurgence of Elijah's mantle?

A Mantle

A mantle, first of all, is a cloak, a covering, and an emblem of authority or power. It denotes an office's insignia of service. The Hebrew word for the prophet's mantle specifically is *addereth*. It comes from the root of their word *addir*. Together the two words mean and inform us of the following things about *mantles* in general, and the *prophet's mantle* in particular.

Quick Study Chart
What a Mantle Is and Does

Addereth and *addir* refer to the *prophet's mantle*, and together mean:

- A covering, a cloak, a garment, a mantle
- A mantle as the source of sustenance, establishment, power, glory, and honor that comes from serving in ministry
- That which causes fame, generates might, and creates worth and nobility as a result of public ministry
- The manifest splendor and magnificence of a delegate, official, or agent of a deity imparted and bestowed as part of the attraction equipment essential to successful service

From the above it is easy to see the prophet's mantle as more than a cloak, or covering. Symbolically, it communicates to the spirit world everything the prophet is and has as a representative of God's kingdom and that he is

His messenger. Thus, the prophet's mantle as a work resource is a power tool, protective garb, an insignia of authority, and emblem of divine license. It is a guard against the elements, a stylized uniform, and statement of service. Its saturation with the Lord's anointing over time, as with Elijah's mantle that Elisha inherited, integrates functional portions of His omniscience, omnipotence, wisdom, counsel, and might. Isaiah 11:1–5 itemizes the qualities and powers inherent in the prophet's mantle, which is a figure of the anointing. What a spiritual mantle's presence upon a person identifies is tantamount to the officer's badge and its radiance. Its density speaks to the wearer's degree of authority and inherent power.

I once ministered to a young woman I had just met. As I began to pray for her and give her the word of the Lord, suddenly right before my eyes there appeared a huge gold badge-shaped shield. It covered her whole chest from shoulder to shoulder and from her neck way past her midsection. Seeing it told me that every vital area of her life was doubly protected by God. I did not know immediately what she did for a living, but the badge, more like a shield, indicated she was a woman of present or future power in God. It was thick and said in essence, "guarded by God." It had taken hits because there were many dents in it, but oddly they were distributed evenly and looked more like engraving than damage. I later learned the woman was of considerable rank in the military. This has happened to me more than once.

On another occasion, I delivered the word of the Lord to a young man, also a stranger to me. Again, I stood before him to prophesy and saw all these occupational signs. I was about to get confused and think, "I can't figure what God wants to focus on with this man." Suddenly in the midst of the panorama of work symbols, an officer's hat appeared. I knew he would be an important person in the military and that in his preordained position, along the way, that he would have ample opportunity to acquire the skills needed to be effective. The path the Lord had him on meant that he would have to do many seemingly odd jobs that appeared unrelated to each other. But ultimately, his experiences would all converge, and once he completed his course he would serve the Lord in high ranking in ministry as well.

As you can see, mantles reflect more than rank in the Creator's service callings. They indicate the learning path of the wearer, the ultimate position, and the assortment of preparatory training skills that would finally comprise the mantle's power and authority. Prophets' mantles signify, using various imagery, their range of ministry and the predecessor their calling descended from, as in the case of Elijah and Elisha, and Elijah and John. The mantle and its condition coincide with the message the prophet concentrates on and the position they hold in the eyes of their sending deity on account of what their predecessor experienced. Sometimes, what is tattered to humans is celebrated by God as triumphant.

Prophets' mantles were more than adornments to decorate them for service. They were viewed as the reflective power of God and so worthy of concrete honor, respect, and reward. When a prophet's word failed or the prophet wanted to be recognized, what distinguished them was the cloak they wore. The coarseness of Elijah's and John's mantles was meant to indicate the harshness of the word they preached and the cost of that word to themselves and their hearers. Isaiah and Ezekiel, two prophets stripped of the customary prophet's mantle, were not exempt from this explanation in that their nakedness represented their message. Their nudeness imaged the outcome of an angry Jehovah who was about to strip His precious country bare. The prophet's symbolism said that its inhabitants would be attired as fugitives instead of kings and priests.

Prophetic Imagery and Symbolism

Aside from knowing the functions of the prophetic office and its diverse manifestations, prophets also need to understand the way God speaks and why. Divine communication often comes in the form of symbolism and imagery. Pictures or signs say visually what is spoken audibly. God is able to speak in all His nations' tongues, but to assure that His word and works are understood in all tongues forever, He uses these two with His agents and workers. Their use is what we mean by the language of the Spirit, and its words are based on His creation. They make the Bible fit age to age.

When the Lord speaks in visions, He uses His own language in the form of imagery. Creation elements and objects visualize God's thoughts. For instance, mountains represent governments, high celestial powers. Hills symbolize high stratospheric powers. River imagery equates to flows and streams as in information or revelation, and trees stand for nations as the Lord's plantings. Chariots exemplify war, and transportation vehicles and horses depict warfare or travel. Symbolic language is necessary for God because it is timeless, transcends time, and tends to apply forever.

Since human language varies from culture to culture, creation symbolism sees to it that what God says over the millennia of earthly existence is always relevant. Think about it. A bird is a bird, known around the world with different names. Winged creatures mean the same thing to every civilization. Likewise, animals, land and water, foliage, dirt, sun, moon, stars, and such all mean the same thing to every generation. God uses them when He wants to depict a human behavior that is analogous with a lower creature, or a spiritual one. It is the same when God uses angelic imagery. Their ordained station is as significant to the message as the creature itself, being heavenly rather than earthly. Weather, family, males, females, and children, regardless of what they are called in a particular country, nonetheless conjure the same image in people's minds. It is for these reasons that imagery serves God's spiritual communication purposes so well around the world era to era. Prophets are very attuned to this reality and are taught by the Lord to grasp what He says no matter what sign or symbol He uses.

Divine symbolism works well in dreams and visions. This is because pictures are self-explanatory and relate to the dreamer's world. Dreamers are instructed by God using images and symbolism typical of their everyday life. When prophetics are at work, since their transmissions are from God, they use His ways of talking to His creatures in their terms. If a trucker is to really heed what the Lord wants to say, then he or she hears God's message in trucking terms. If the word comes in a vision, the Lord captures their attention by using highway, road stop, or payload imagery. In like manner, if the Lord needs to get a cook's attention, He will use food, recipes, cookware, and utensils as well as hungry or satisfied eaters.

Visions are a little different from dreams. They are more like broadcasts that depict the mind and happenings of God in His expressions irrespective of our comprehension. Visions tell God's story God's way, and leave their interpretation and translation to the recipient to obtain from His Spirit. Visions are not interested in our trends, idioms, slang, or language. Many times they appear outdated. The Lord resorts to contemporary terms when they help Him make His point. Otherwise, the words and terms He uses are drawn from the things He made, the earth, the heavens, the air, water, and so forth. Good prophetic training says the prophet must become adept at God's wording. To see that they do, the Lord begins them in a study of His prophet's writings. He walks them through the words He spoke long ago and causes them to zero in on His own interpretations. Once the prophet gets the hang of this, he or she is ready for more advanced lessons in symbology.

In the next chapter, the ancient premise for modern prophetics is presented.

Chapter 4

RESIDENT PROPHET MINISTRY ORIGIN

Early Pattern of Church Prophet

This chapter talks about the ancient Eastern patterns of the *nabi* institutions that mirror the New Testament church prophet. According to historic accounts, as alluded to above, the concept of a resident or stationary prophet devoted to the spiritual and supernatural best interests of a single group or entity is dated. Long before Israel came into existence, the practice flourished as a custom in the ancient Near East. The very term used for the prophet's institution is derived from them. It is the term *nabiim,* from which we get our present use of the word *nabi* discussed earlier. The greatest order of institutionalized prophets came from the Mari prophets of old. They are credited with the framework and forms of prophetic ministry that devolved in Israel.

For Mari, having dedicated prophets on hand in the civil courts and sanctuaries of the land was a must. Their highly developed spirituality warranted it. They would not have thought of engaging in anything significant without prophetic counsel. The stationary prophet was a ruling class in their day, and many of them were organized into ministry companies or organized guilds. Although the influence they wielded was mainly supernatural, it was nonetheless strongly felt throughout society. *Nabi* power and wisdom was regarded as pivotal to any consequential event by all in authority.

Mari leaders apart from the advice, perceptions, and supernatural investigations of the resident prophet did nothing. It is their Amorite pattern perfected by Babylon that the Israelite followed in instituting and ultimately refining its own order. After all, Abraham was a Babylonian prophet. To appreciate the need for today's resident prophet, one must look to the pattern cultivated by these institutions. From it came the Philistine prophets, the prophets of Ashdod, the Amorites, and the most infamous prophetic institution of Israel—that of Baal of Tyre, over which the Phoenician queen Jezebel ruled. All these prophetic classes received their guidelines for professional prophetics from these models.

Under the primitive Mari institution, prophets above all mediated the supernatural. It was their voice that auditioned the moods, will, and dispositions of the gods of the land. They also acted out the outcomes of the nation's critical events in theatrical exhibitions. For instance, in times of war they demonstrated the strategy of the enemy and the counterattacks of the god they represented. Ahab's staff of resident prophets demonstrate this in action in 1 Kings 22.

As functionaries of the supernatural sphere of the territories they guarded, the prophets issued rulings and decrees that set up and deposed kings, overturned the edicts of governments, and perpetuated their orders by identifying and preparing future prophets to succeed them. They handled dream interpretation and performed classic seer functions. The *nabiim*, beyond this, performed clairvoyant and divination activities to read the future. It seems their most essential function was to learn the future, apply it to the present, and then orchestrate—through prophesying and simulation—the events that would bring their word to pass. Read the prophet who declared that Josiah the king would be born and overturn the vile institution crafted by Jeroboam in 1 Kings 13.

Unlike the later prophetics of the Greeks, after which most of the New Testament church prophetics are patterned, the *nabiim* of old were more than mere mouthpieces. They were potent visionaries, adept statesmen and diplomats, and sentient ambassadors of the spirit realm. They appear throughout history as extraordinary tacticians and warriors. Their presence, it was believed, possessed the ability to sway the balance of power wherever there was a contest between themselves and the gods of foreign lands. Such was the case with Elijah's Mount Carmel contest with Ahab and Jezebel's prophetic staff.

Without question, the Mari-Babylon *nabi* was expected to do more than utter a prophetic word. This agent of the supernatural was expected to exercise the powers that inspired the utterance as well. In doing so, the *nabi* moved the spirits and forces of creation to act and so forced their word's materialization. Those who could not do so received the reputation as a false prophet. Deuteronomy 13 shows the Lord admonishing Israel about them, saying that if their words did not come to pass they were not to be feared. The Mari prophets and other ancient followers of their pattern operated the supernatural, positioned its alliance, and assured the god who spoke through them became renowned for its power. Hence a good amount of spiritual and supernatural intervention, mediation, and maneuvering was at the disposal of this agent.

Being a professional class of their society meant the *nabiim* were treated as regularly compensated staff by those they served. In addition, they were, as compensated professionals, on call under these conditions at the behest of royalty, nobility, and priests of their precincts. Their rank presupposed the status of the entity they served. If the arrangement was a new one, it was the *nabi* who elevated the status and thus the spiritual control of the entity that engaged them. This was true if the entity was the government, the entire nation, or a sanctuary. By this it is meant that a well-known, highly prized prophet could correspondingly elevate the site to which he or she was assigned.

From the above, the model for what today's prophets are to do is clear. Israel no doubt had access to this information and used it as a foundation for the ministry that eventually took over the spirituality of the land. Moses knew it when he led and established the country, based on the experience he no doubt gained while in training in Egypt's track to kingship, and intensified in lessons from Jethro. Both settings more than educated him in the office of the prophet, the supernatural, and all the gods that the two countries worshipped. That Moses well understood this is seen in Exodus 18 when he met Jethro in the wilderness after God brought them out of Israel. He understood his work as the nation's prophet and began to carry it out alone until Jethro corrected him.

Although Israel knew all about such things, they did not entirely throw their knowledge away. What the country did, however, was endeavor to purge from their prophetic ordinances and orders the occultic and demonic so their supernatural work would be hallowed for Jehovah. Here is why the Lord did not have to tell them what a prophet was or did. Moses could say to Jethro what he was doing because he well understood the role and work of the prophet in a land. Only the stubborn areas of divination, prognostication, and augury from the ancient models refused to be purged or permanently shunned. Throughout the life of the land, these continued to infiltrate Israel's prophetics.

A similar danger lurks to spoil every generation's prophetics today because Satan invariably seeks to recover lost ground by duplicating what the Lord does and masking the duplication with humanism. He needs the prophetic voices and spirits of God's prophets to do so expeditiously. This is what Jeremiah 23 means when it says the false prophets steal the Lord's words.

How Israel's Prophetic Order Began

The Bible tells us when and how Israel's official prophetics became an established institution in the principality of God. It was at the dawn of

Samuel's tenure. He was the first prophet under the Mosaic kingdom to institutionalize the order. Taking, presumably, his pattern for the institution from what was in existence in his day and that which predated his country's prophetics, Samuel set out to refine the ministry to serve the Lord. By now we know that would be the ancient *nabi* that officiated over the centuries every nation's religious history. Every religion, it seems, had its prophet, seer, shaman, priest-craft, healer, and teacher that administrated its supernatural resources and mediated its access to it. These, it would seem, comprised the fundamental elements of a religion regardless of the god it was created to serve.

Consequently, the priest being established and the prophetic having been initiated by Moses in Israel's deliverance, it was Samuel who was chosen to supply the remainder of the kingdom's spiritual components. Samuel also inaugurated the judgeship system under the direction and rule of Jehovah. In respect to the *nabis* of old, present chronicles show that only Israel's prophets rose to lasting renown and became the enduring standard of the prophetic for modern man. Their words are still active today and many readers can attest that they came to pass or are yet coming to pass.

Although Joshua was considered a prophet, his service was mainly militaristic as the kingdom had yet to be established in Israel's control. Until that time, however, the priests using the Urim and Thummim answered prophetic revelation on spontaneous issues and questions requiring God's answers. Of course, this excludes the supernatural manipulation by the occultic prophets such as Balaam that dominated the ancient world at the time. Accepted and respected as a social order, the demonic ministrations of the supernatural that preceded Israel's prophetic institution held largely uncontested sway. The first stunning challenge it received came from Moses in his deliverance of the nation of God from Egyptian bondage. See 1 Samuel 3:1. It talks about how widespread revelation was rare in those days.

By the time Samuel was old enough to serve the Lord, Eli's sons' perversion of the priesthood and rank abuse of God's people paved the way for a division of the two functions, the priest and the prophet. Furthermore, their defilement of God's offerings in the process forever settled the separate operations of the two offices according to 1 Samuel 1–3. Their repugnant behavior caused the people to fear Eli's death and resist his sons' dynastic inheritance of the priesthood.

The combined resentment of the people over the sometimes violent abuse they suffered at the hands of Eli's sons set the stage for God's final division of His two spiritual powers. The wisdom of the principle may be better appreciated by looking at Ecclesiastes 5:8. The priesthood, being deformed, had no higher official to oversee it. God's disillusioned people had no human recourse to appeal to outside of Eli, who had already refused to discipline his offspring. Samuel's progenies did little to alter their state of mind on this later down the line. When his service was nearing an end, his unruly sons revived Israel's earlier fears.

The people again questioned the character of leadership they would get from Samuel's sons. By the time he passed the institution of the *nabiim* on, the two functions had permanently split.

The Lord Balances His Spiritual Powers

To create and maintain a godly balance of power, the Lord always groups His hierarchical officials in varying levels of ministers that oversee each other. That is what Ecclesiastes 5:8 means. This structure allows them to rectify abuses and inequities in His kingdom, and it is not exclusive to the church. Such was the case with Eli, Samuel, the prophetic, and the priesthood.

To assure the revelatory provisions of God were not monopolized by one lone group, the Lord distributed spiritual power among the two existing official revelatory institutions He ordained in that day, the priest and the prophet respectively.

Bible accounts indicate God's prophetics as a ministry that had been practically muted in the nation's developing institutions from the time of Moses to Samuel. The end of Joshua's era also ended the fixture of established prophetics and the godly use of spiritual power. Divine utterances were loosely delivered by whatever prophet was available. The priesthood curtailed the legal exercise of God's supernatural exploits to their personal advantage. Their dominance caused the prophetic to fade into the background, eventually becoming nostalgic window dressing on the nation's spiritual landscape.

Priestly ministry, concurrent with this move, rapidly became presumptuous. The young nation's secular, political, and social dominions each took their natural courses and shapes as Israel grew. Only the prophetic remained fetal in nature. It alone lagged behind as an important professional class in Israel's culture, blending with the priests' teaching mandates, and became locked into their interpretations and applications. Spontaneous utterances were rare because they were hindered and eventually suffocated. The manipulations of Eli's sons reflect this. See 1 Samuel 1–2.

Since no concrete provisions were left by Moses to found and extend his prophetic initiatives into the cultural life of the new nation, the priests developed the function as they wanted. Moses had made, however, provisions for the prophetic's eventual reinstitution in Exodus 18. Nevertheless, he prepared no definite guidelines for its emergence among the ranks of the Lord's officers. It took God's displeasure with Eli's ministry and His judgment on his immoral priesthood to change all that, and He did so with Samuel. God instigated the new move spearheaded by Samuel that would perpetually have both prophet and priest regulating each other.

To introduce His change, in response to the nation's degeneration, God sent an unnamed prophet with a word to Eli the high priest. He declared that both Eli and his posterity would be permanently obliterated because of the depravity he endorsed in the land. Not long after this, the Lord awakened the prophet Samuel's spirit to undertake the mandate of *institutionalizing* the prophetic. His charge included restoring Israel's pure worship and perpetually guarding against the potential excesses of the priests in the future. See 1 Samuel 3.

Samuel the Priestly Prophet

The task of instating a standing moral council of prophetic officers was given to one born expressly for that purpose. Samuel's very name says so. It means "name of God" or "God's name" to show how his work would again exalt the name of the Lord in the lifestyle and worship of His people. It is noteworthy to point out how the Lord chose Samuel for the judgeship.

Providentially called to be a prophet and to restore the nation's worship to its covenant God, Samuel was reared by a priest in the tabernacle of God. The young man was equally well learned in all his assigned callings. He was knowledgeable of the ministries of the priesthood, nurtured as a prophet and judge, and groomed for governmental leadership at once. Thus, Samuel would be both separator and bridge in the nation's new move. His appointment would paradoxically merge and divide its priestly and prophetic functions for integrity and efficiency. As Israel's first judge, he functioned symmetrically as Israel's priest, prophet, and governor.

Samuel's appointment first closed out the priesthood's terrorist reign as supreme power in the land. He then ushered in the joint reign of prophet and priest under the interim reign system of judgeship that preceded Israel's shift to monarchy. Deborah, in Judges 5, was the only other *prophet* accredited like authority. She performed all the functions Samuel did in her service, acting as commander and chief, as well as gubernatorial prophet in the land. Ascribing the title judge to Deborah's office gave her the same authority and status Samuel enjoyed. A complete portrait of his ministry provides a credible service model for today's prophets assigned to individual churches.

Samuel's Mantle: A Church Prophet Ministry Model

Samuel's mantle of judge, prophet, and priest comprised the transition team of that era that concluded the old order, regulated priestly authority, and installed a new institution at the same time. His first official act was to issue the decrees that judged Eli's house, broke Israel's ties with the occult, and established himself and his order as her head of state. Following this, Samuel taught the nation about holy and unholy service and corrected the errors of the priest's ministry. Samuel meticulously reeducated Israel about the office of the prophet and elevated its previously incidental function to an official rank in the ministries of the Lord's land.

Samuel led Israel to war as a captain, arbitrated their controversies as a judge, instructed them in divine service and worship as a priest, and established a school to structure and standardize their prophetics. Samuel's work extending to inaugurating the royalty and nobility of the land, qualifying subsequent prophets, and verifying and empowering new leaders and officers with God's approved authority.

One thing is evident is this profile, Samuel pointedly depicts the diverse functions and activities of the prophet installed in a church more than any of his predecessors. He was a commander in war, an intercessor in covenant breaches, and officiator at all the nation's ceremonies. From this, it is easy to see the question of dedicated prophets assigned to every congregation for God is not strictly a matter of wisdom. It is an ordination that goes all the way to the heart of necessity, seeing to it that every gathering of God's people in His name reflects the full complement of His officers and agencies. It allows the Lord to manifest and demonstrate His fullness when He is with His people. If a ministry wants to become and remain biblically correct, then every gathering is to contain a representative of four out of five of the Ephesians 4:11 officers. The apostle as founder may be itinerant as well as the evangelist. In addition, church gatherings, based on 1 Corinthians 14:19–32, should have in attendance a minimum of two to three prophetic voices. God's integrity and diligence says that there usually are, even if they are not allowed to speak out in service.

Benefit of Church Prophets in Every Church

If a church and its leadership want to succeed in their vision and divine mandate, then opening itself up to the credible prophetics of God is a good start. If that church wishes to excel in its purpose and ride the crest of sustained victory, establishing its own church or resident prophets is how to do it.

Before going further, I want to acknowledge that many people object to the title "church prophet." For those who do, the term *resident prophet,* or *staff* or *sanctuary prophet* works just as well. Regardless of the name you use, the title applies to prophets of congregations whose main duties and spheres of influence concentrate on a local church and its congregation(s). They are likely to be your shepherding prophets, more than anything else. Our discussion here is not addressing itinerant prophets serving a number of churches in a circuit, much like the one Samuel traveled. Here our attention is given to one in a church called to the prophetic, or sent by God to become the prophet of the church. Since not everyone is called to the national or international realms of the prophet's office, it is wise to deduce those assigned to other levels are called to cover individual churches and ministries.

Church prophets as an ordained institution spiritually, and sometimes practically, guard and protect local congregations. They also, when requested, provide the same benefit for various itinerant ministers. Under these circumstances, their function acts more like a mentorship.

In the local congregation, the prophet's ministries are mostly limited to exercising the Lord's authority in the work they are assigned to and locally releasing His power from the world of the supernatural to enhance it. The ever-present spiritual strength of the Lord is what the church prophet brings to the local church. His or her presence assures pastor and congregation alike reap to the full the new covenant blessings promised every New Creation child of God in the Lord Jesus Christ; the very thing Satan and his hosts seek to deprive the churches and their membership of. Prophets bring balance to the prophetic expressions that flow through the church. Furthermore, they add a fuller dimension of spirituality to routine prophetic service customarily handled by whosoever will.

Moreover, these officers standardize the proprieties of the office and regulate its practices and developments. Well trained and seasoned staff or resident prophets being competence and prophetic mastery to the churches they serve. When operated in harmony with the other ministries of the church, the accomplished prophet can swiftly elevate their church's rank in the spiritual realm. Easily they can ignite increases in resources and release previously held up funds to flow into the church. Their intercessions can reduce community hostility, win the favor of civil authorities, and disarm principalic agents working against the ministry. Besides this, the church prophet can overall enrich the spiritual and natural state of the ministry in areas too numerous to mention here.

Regulating the Prophetic

As wide-scale prophetics are relatively new to this generation, its organization is ever evolving as a valid church institution. Finding its reputable place among the five-fold officers of the New Testament church, and establishing its parameters and protocol is a massive ongoing venture. Here lays the ground for sound prophetic *guidelines*. They are intended to steer the processes pastors use to install prophetics in their churches.

To help you perceive the official nature of the prophet's rank and the mantle's status as an office, a discussion of the prophet's standing in the supernatural is in order. We start with the link between the prophetic and an agency in the next chapter.

Chapter 5

THE PROPHETIC'S AGENCY STATUS

The Prophetic—An Official Agency of the Godhead

All study on this subject points to the status of the prophetic as an agency. The word agency defines a business and its operations. An agency is an official entity that administrates and executes the duties and responsibilities associated with a delegation, usually called a commission. *Official* is a key term as it asserts order, permanence, perpetuity, and solidarity as the result of an agency arrangement.

The attachment of the word *official* to anything means it is backed by a governing power authorized by a higher one to support, oversee, and police the activities of the agency. This role includes the guarantee of its agreements and the warranty of its services and provisions. To add this definition to the function of a commission sheds a great light on what the prophetics is and means to God.

The word *commission* is used regularly in scripture to designate those who are sent out on an errand for a specific purpose by one in authority. The distinctive of the commission over the errand runner or routine messenger is the authority that accompany the dispatch. To be recognized as an agency, the idea of a delegated commission must be real.

A commission, broadly speaking, is an authoritative power-wielding entity that rules or governs subordinate entities. Commissions are born when the originating powers or forces that initiated the movement, business, or activities that necessitate an agency, hands down portions of its activities to delegates to represent its interests. Those who are commissioned are charged with prescribed duties. When we speak of a delegation in the context of agency service or commissioned action, its meaning is larger than what is customarily understood in routine work circles. An official delegation service is much broader and carries infinitely more weight. It includes deputation and an assignment under an authority. Just take a moment to study those words and you will see what is really meant by the term delegation.

God's Divine Communications Media

The prophetic is a divine agency of the Godhead. It is how the Lord God keeps in contact with His world. His uniqueness is that instead of telephones, headsets, wires, and satellites, the Lord uses dreams and visions and angelic visitations from the spiritual creatures assigned to the planet. As the Creator's eternal communications media, the prophetic doubles as an effective administrative instrument. Through prophecy God dispenses His truth, enlightens His people, and issues His judgments in the earth. Prophecy declares God's plans and actuates His words and will in their seasons. All this makes it so much more than a predictive tool, establishing it as His rod of correction, staff of rulership, and creative implement. With these, prophecy also acts like a trigger mechanism with signals that call into action the embedded commands of the Lord dormant in creation until their time. The greatest example of this is the Revelation of the apostle John. The entire event unfolded to him by Christ's angel is but a series of prophetic spurs that rouse and initialize the words of God asleep in creation until their times.

Prophecy is how God extends His hands to the world and causes what He wants to appear in it to do so on time. Thus it further serves as His inducement arm. The Old Testament word for ministry used in Hosea 12:10 links prophecy to the hand of God, translating the word ordinarily used for hand (*yad*) as ministry. Together, all this says that prophecy is the Lord's means of invoking the powers and agencies responsible for exteriorizing His word and manifesting His power and will in action on earth.

Beyond this, the prophetic serves as God's avenue of divine enactment and legislation, according to Galatians 3:19 and Hebrews 2:2. As an instrument that invokes the terrestrial agencies, angels, and powers of creation, prophets participate in their summons via the medium of prophecy. See Ezekiel 9:1–11 and Zechariah 3:1–10. Other words for agent are listed below to give you an idea of the scope of the function in the mind of God and any legitimate organization. An agent is:

- Executive
- Administrator
- Judge
- President
- Minister
- General
- Chairperson
- Governor
- Guardian
- Custodian
- Prelate

Agents and Officers—What They Do

In relation to the prophet, agents as officers exercise and exert the delegated authority they derive from the Godhead. Based on the language of 1 Corinthians 12:28–29, prophets govern by ruling and administration beneath God's sovereignty. Ideally, they do so according to His divine

canon (written law). Aside from legislation, prophets organize the operations and structure of the New Testament church, taking part in its discipline as indicated: corrective, instructive, or punitive. The instructional
mandate typical of prophets in general and church prophets in particular
further requires the prophet's mantle to be apt to teach.

Advancing the reasons for the office's continuance, prophets still judge
according to the Lord's word of truth, manage His executive administrative affairs, supervise those in their care, and guard the body of Christ
against demonic infiltration or worldly overflows. As ministers, they develop the saints in Christ's spirituality, officiate over its priestly tasks in
the earth, and enforce the righteousness of God. As protectors and servants, prophets cover, shield, and encircle their congregations, interceding for them as necessary.

Intercede is a word that many people only partially understand. Besides praying for someone, it means to intervene in their matters with
one's own authority and position, invoking God's influence while doing
so. Zephaniah 2:7 (NKJV) applies this word to a special divine visitation
where God acts on behalf of His people as the word of a qualified agent.
Prophetic prayer performs just this function. When one intercedes for
another, they are actually interposing themselves between the victim and
their problems or crises. Prophets, as God's intercessors, first and fore-
most accomplish exploits of that kind in their prayers and combat for the
churches they cover. See Jeremiah 15:1 and Ezekiel 14:14. Both passages
show God's regard for the prophet's intercessory prayer on behalf of His
people.

In addition, practically and economically speaking, the prophet dis-
burses God's economy as we have seen from 2 Chronicles 20:20, and
dispenses His covenant provisions to them. Often overlooked is the practical meaning of the word dispensation as used in the New Testament.
Along with its referring to a period of time, it also means stewardship
over the economy of a household. Thus, the prophet's powerful status in

the realms and spheres of God authorize the release of the resources and possessions hidden in His and His other creatures' treasuries. An interesting fact about all this is that every worker in God's kingdom has their own treasury in eternity from which streams the supernatural supplies of their service. Each minister is given a storehouse of weapons, finances, abilities, and skills with which they serve God and meet the needs of His people. Prophets' treasuries are usually quite stocked. This is because they are to release and dispense great portions of it to those who come to them. More than material blessings, the prophet's mantle contains spiritual and miraculous resources that overturn everything the devil and his angels may throw at those they surround. When Christ gave His instructions to the twelve apostles before their first missionary journey in Matthew 10, what He released in their spheres of ministry was powerful. Likewise, Elijah and Elisha were both so endowed. Elisha knew that Elijah's mantle was both powerful and wealthy. Therefore, he understood that he was getting more than a cloak or a uniform. He recognized that all the power and benefits that ever streamed from Elijah were resident in that hairy garment. When he asked for the mantle, he knew that it would more than cover him; it would transform, empower, and enrich his life and service to God as long as he lived. Had he only gotten a word from Elijah or the laying on of hands, he would not have been nearly as potent in his ministry. The power that remained in that mantle is revealed through the Bible's record of Elisha's early exploits in 2 Kings.

Prophets as Agents

Prophets, like all the five-fold officers of Ephesians 4:11, are officers and that makes them agents. The prophetic as a divine agency makes those who stand in the position or even those who are used from time to time by the Lord to bring forth a prophetic word, agents. By now you well understand an agent is a representative of a principal, usually a sovereign land, monarch, or government. Agents and their agencies serve as ambassadors, consuls, delegates, intermediaries, and the like. When you think of the prophet and the prophecies that come from the messenger's mouth, recognize that their position with the Lord authorizes their words and assures their performance. It is their license from God that frees them to exercise His power, enforce His will, and perform (or cause the performance of) His word.

A prophet of God, as His agent, transacts the Lord's business the same way an agent of an insurance company or other entity does. As a recognized representative in good standing, a companies' agents, according to their contracts, bind their organizations to the performance of their word. So long as prophets obey the Lord's word and respect the bounds and limits of their ministry covenant, the prophecies they give cannot fail. Understand that exteriorizing the Lord's spoken word in the natural world is not only how prophets are so designated, but is emblematic of their fundamental reason for existing. If God does not honor a prophet's word or substantiate the messenger's work, then the person is not a prophet in actuality, at least not yet, or until then.

The key to prophetic honor is the prophet's words. They consistently come to pass proving the deity they represent backs them in all professional regards. This requisite alone already ordains that prophetic preeminence takes time because new prophets' prophecies can take awhile to come to pass. The time lag between a prophecy and its fulfillment can make people not accept them as a prophet for years. I have had people contact me, or have run into people five or more years after that fact that I have given a word to. They confess they did not receive my word at the time, or rejected it as just me. What amazes them after so many years is that the words I spoke, regardless of their reaction to them, were performed by God. What amazes me is that He not only performed my word in time, but He let them know that it was according to the prophecy I gave that He did so. This ought to encourage many young prophets. Be patient because matters of life take time, and even if you know your word was right on when you gave it, rest in the fact that God will confirm you. The idea that prophetic confirmation is always a quick event is misleading. Sometimes, part of your training is in the waiting.

Why Agencies and Agents Exist

An agency exists to administrate the affairs of the commission, bureau, or business that brought it into existence. It expedites its affairs, executes its commands, exercises its authority, and accomplishes its purposes and aims as prescribed in the agency agreement. As instruments (one synonym for the word agent) or principals, agencies are empowered by their principal to intervene on their behalf, intercede for their best interests, and direct and govern their affairs. What an explanation. Prophets, then, are to see to God's business and not their own. Their words are to uphold and expedite God's purpose for sending them and not what they want to be. Prophets must become aware that they are God's agents and their ministries, His divine agency.

Their agency is ordinarily interposed in the territory of the principal or settled in a remote territory amid the population it exists to serve. Its call is to establish the principal's authority and strengthen its holdings in distant lands. Think about how the prophetic is to accomplish this on behalf of the Godhead and the kingdom of heaven on earth. As with natural or secular agents, so it is with God's spiritual ones. Prophets are assigned by the Lord to territories over which they rule and spheres of ministry within which they serve. In ecclesiastical matters, prophetic delegation and dispatch pertain to the church's realm on earth. Prophets under these circumstances become the embodiment of God's executive authority.

Extent of Agency Power and Authority

The word *authority* means the lawful right to enforce obedience, the legitimate power to influence or direct the behavior of others—usually subordinates. The exercise of authority involves instruction, command, censure, and discipline. Hebrew terms for *authority* convey words and sentiment that ascribe majesty, glory, honor, renown, even ornamentation to our basic understanding of the word. These all signify the exalted station of one placed in authority over others. Additional words and meanings confer the accompanying grandeur, appearance, and excellency that impose their forms upon the one so installed. The sum of these words explains the weight of authority and its affects on those upon whom it is placed.

It is not difficult to see how, based on the above, authority originated with God; nor is it hard to understand its effect in Moses' inauguration of Joshua, one example of prophetic authority at work. As a matter of fact, whenever Moses was instructed by God about inaugurating anyone, he was told to take of the authority that was upon himself in the form of the spirit, and place it upon the inaugurated one. Here is the spiritual significance behind the laying on of hands in ceremonial promotions and appointments. The goal of the act is the impartation of the spiritual properties of the promoter through the delegation. Once completed, the act is seen by heaven to transfer or transmit agency authority on the one touched. That impartation invests a person with the power of the office into which they step.

Agency authority extends to setting and enforcing laws and mandating prescribed behaviors. This consists of permitting and disallowing certain acts perceived by the delegated representative to be harmful, detrimental, or nullifying to his or her principal's best interests. Agency guardianship extends to the agent's assurance of the institution's perpetuity. Thus, the agency as the delegated command authority is to sway and influence its realms, territories, and regions to the advantage of the commissioning principal.

The Agency Principal

An agency cannot be very legitimate without the head person who ordained its existence. That head person supplies the agency's authority. The name for such a person we have said is a principal. A principal is a chief or head that empowers the agent and agency to act and speak on his or her behalf. As a principal, he or she initiates and governs the delegates charged with carrying on business and administrating its vision in its name. This is a commission, a term particularly applicable when more than tasks and assignments are involved in the sending.

The principal is first in the line of power in a delegated arrangement. As such, he or she is the ranking authority that inspires, authorizes, and endorses the agency and all that it discharges. Moses' inauguration of Joshua to succeed him exemplified this type of delegation in action, as did Christ's empowering and dispatch of the twelve. Moses' transference of power delegated like authority at the direct command of the Lord, who may be seen as the sending principal of the Israel project. See Numbers 27:23.

When the Lord inducts and dispatches His prophets, He does so as a principal and makes the prophets, indeed all His ministers, functionaries representing Him in the world. For a heightened respect of the prophetic and all the ministries of the New Testament church, adequate enlightenment must be given to their charges who are to see their orders as delegated commands from the Lord.

Besides sending, principals are persons and groups who authorize, underwrite, and guarantee their agencies' right to exist, to do business, and to legally act in their remote territories. The verifying factor is that the one who delegated the authority and who sponsored the agency must have sovereign power and/or lawful jurisdiction within the territory the agency serves. A principal, as one in authority (a person or nation), spearheads the actions or movements that generated the agency's presence in the land. The Bible calls them heads (*arche* or *archon* in the Greek).

Agency Principal Relationship

True agencies are accountable to their principals first. They hold to his or her dominant views and ideals on the mission, its assignments, tasks, operations, and duties. The agreement between the principal and agent, ideally, extends to the best means of carrying out these for the principal as well. The four, mission, assignments, tasks, and duties, are all integral to an agency. Without them the organization and its institutions have no basis to practice. Agencies' remote administration and government, along with their workers, called agents, therefore are illegal. Activities conducted under these circumstances may be construed as anarchic and dissenting without a lawful principal. This can also be the case when the principal has failed to define for the agency its parameters. Apart from them, the legitimacy needed for agency occupation is absent.

Here is where the prophetic receives its legitimacy. Christ, being the head of the church and the Lord over creation, gives the prophet his or her legitimate right to act in all the world. It is His authority that is delegated to, and exercised by the prophet, not their own as many suppose. *The prophet as an agent of the Godhead* is to pursue the content of the delegation handed down by Christ. Although that delegation is mainly spiritual, the reality of certain consequences for dereliction spans the Bible. What gives most prophets their boldness against the Lord is their shortsighted self-will. Such prophets believe the Lord has little recourse for their disobedience and have become too familiar with His longsuffering grace, and take liberties not accorded to them. These messengers see God as out of sight, and therefore out of mind and control. However, the Lord has dealt with this before, according to Psalm 94:7.

Since the rewards and penalties for service to God presumably come later, many ministers feel they can take what they want now and bear the consequences later. Scripture, however, tells us that is not always the case. See Matthew 7:13 and the Lord's parabolic contrast to the good and faithful servant versus the evil and faithless servant.

The Agency Agent

It is the agency's founding or initiating principals who commission them as authorized representatives for a discrete purpose. The commission is the embodiment of what defines the agency's work. It encapsulates the purpose for its dispatch, delegated authority, and authorizes their business, services, and dispensations as related to the founding purpose. All must be clearly defined for the operative or functionary (two other synonyms for agent) to complete their assignments. Because agency assignments are usually apart from their principal's residence or headquarters location, the word dispatch heads the list of what a commission entails.

The sending away aspect of the assignment requires principal deputation that sanctions the commission and its agency representatives. In written and notarized documents, the principal states how the agency is to legally perform in their name in distant territories. It is the power of the commission that gives the dispatched (sent ones) the permission to execute the commands and charges of the principal as defined. An agent, as a representative of the commissioner, acts as an instrument employed by the principal to virtually be the principal away from the hub or headquarters location. Prophets are equated to Christ as long as He is in heaven, as seen by the Lord's words to Moses in Exodus 7:1.

Legitimate Commissioning

One important thing worth mentioning about a commission is the present-day church's acts of commissioning. The church has taken up the practice of nonchalantly laying hands on people in informal ceremonies to *commission* them to go forth. To what or where are not always defined. Such a practice under certain circumstances done in the name of Jesus is not inherently wrong. It can, however, be dangerous. Casual acts of commissioning can be somewhat misleading and can activate spiritual forces and warfare the newly commissioned one is not prepared to confront. This is especially true when the person commissioned has had little preparatory training and minuscule information on the nature, purpose, and aim of their commission. To perform the ritual as merely a religious service only strips it of its powerful inaugural impartation.

For the commissioner to have power to dispatch agents, the factors stated above must be established. The commissioner must be a legitimate principal. He or she must have sovereign or legal authority within the realm of the commission to be economically, spiritually, or otherwise able to support the agent—the one on whom hands are laid for dispatch. Thus, the commissioner must be above or at least more highly endowed than the one being sent forth. The reason for this has to do with the sure difficulties, hardships, and obstacles the agent will face while on assignment.

The commissioner should be able to finance, shelter, protect, and extend his or her reach (and aid) to encircle the agent. He or she should be more than capable of undergirding the remote agent's activities in the distant territory. There must be sufficient license to authorize, anointing to empower and impart, and resources to sustain the operative in the remote location. These possessions demand the commissioner be more than a peer or subordinate.

The commissioning body's word, moreover, should be respected and heeded in the place where the agent is sent. The legitimacy of the commission and the reputation of the commissioner have to be impeccable for the agent to effectively serve or have the power to enforce the principal's commands. Additionally, a certifying letter attesting to the legitimacy of the agent and the authenticity of the commission is necessary. Study for insight the account of Peter, and the other apostles' dispatch of Paul to his ministry to the Gentiles in the book of Galatians. Review also their reception of him when he was brought to them by Barnabas for the first time. Re-examine as well their protective escort of Paul when the Jewish authorities sought to kill him for his defection to Christ. All these examples show the principal must have the status in the natural and supernatural realms to assure the agent's survival and success.

The official rank of the principal or commissioner (sometimes this authority is delegated) must legally and practically exceed that of the agent. Principals must have jurisdiction in the assigned territory for the acts and the dispensations of their commissioned ones, agents, to be official. Officialdom is significant to an authentic commission. Those employed by an agency are its officials as the words *officers* and *agents* too are synonymous.

Being an official also makes the agent an intermediary who bridges negotiation and settlement gaps as an envoy or deputy who transacts business for the principal. He or she, in this stead, forms diplomatic ties between the two in a distant location. This statement is significant as distance, remote government, and management are integral to most agencies purposes. In this way, the agent doubles as ambassador on the principal's behalf. One synonym for the word ambassador is *minister*. This word brings the subject of our discussion to the church and shows how the preceding explanations pertain to the prophetic.

You see, prophetics are second-ranking *officers* of the five-fold ministry unfolded by Paul in the book of Ephesians 4:11 and 1 Corinthians 2:28. As officers of the church, they are immediately ministers of Christ's gospel and its legitimate power agents.

Agent and Agency Role in the Church

In the church, a minister is a servant of God. As His servant, the minister fills one of two roles. He or she can be a lay servant who serves the Lord, though not necessarily in an administrative, governmental, or executive capacity, or he or she can be an officer. The latter term applies to the Ephesians 4:11 positions outlined by the apostle Paul. Their names make them officers with agency authority and responsibilities.

Being sent by the Lord Jesus certifies their service as a dispatch or a commission. For our purposes, this discussion centers on the latter defi-

nition, that being, the officer of the five-fold offices. Official fits because
to be in an office intrinsically makes one an officer. First Corinthians
12:28–29 settles this for us, as does an etymological study of the term
and application of the word *officer.*

The Agent as an Officer

An officer can apply to an executive or director, a manager or a vice, a
general or a chief. If you studied these thoroughly, you would immediately see *the prophet as an agent of the Godhead, and his or her service (or
ministry) an agency of the kingdom of God.* These conclusions are reached
from the sum of the explanatives given earlier for the term *agent.* Prophets, along with the other Ephesians 4:11 officers, do in the spirit realm
supernaturally for the Lord and His kingdom what diplomatic, civil, and
political authorities do for their earthly organizations.

Prophets administrate the heavenly treasures of the New Creation
government. They officially handle the dispensations of the supernatural
released by God in His church. Prophets, further, exercise the Lord's spiritual authority on earth to keep the balance of power between the darkness and light, the truth and the lie. They authorize and empower the
church's ministries and supply God's heavenly provisions to His people
by decreeing and declaring what the Lord gives them to dispense.

As agencies of the Godhead, prophetic officers are licensed to maintain God's control and communicate His divine approval and good fortune to the body of Christ; again, not unlike what earthly agents do for
their agencies. They stabilize, advance, and enlarge the kingdom of God
and manage official kingdom ventures on His behalf. Prophets execute
their commission, charges, discharges, and duties as commanded by the
Lord using primarily His word, spontaneous, written, and revealed.

What makes this essential knowledge for the advancement of the
prophetic is its realm of application. The prophetic agency is one of the
many powers of the kingdom that establishes strongholds for the Lord

Jesus Christ. The totality of these strongholds, along with their powers and forceful authorities, constitute the church's grounding as His ordained principality according to Ephesians 1:15–23. Prophetic wards are set up to stream God's eternal light and divine truth into the world to reverse death and overturn its edicts in the lives of those touched by it. As the power force of the Lord's lone earthly principality, prophets are to see that His churches profit and not bankrupt the planet.

Prophetic Agency an Outgrowth of God's Principality

A principality is the territory of a prince's dominion. It is the sphere of domain and authority of the offspring of a king. The offspring, in so far as God is concerned, are His born-again children. As His servants, they most specifically are the church officers Ephesians 4:11 identifies. The church's instatement as God's eternal principality reversed the coupe Satan pulled off in the Garden of Eden with Adam, who surrendered his position as head of God's ancient principalities. Since then they have, up to Christ, been world dominated or manipulated. The sons of darkness have held sway over the main of the world's holdings. Only when the supernatural forces of God in the spirit realm merge with the vessels of His Spirit on earth is the balance of supernatural power affected. Refer back to our discussion of God's spiritual protocratics. Also, see Daniel 10:21; Ezekiel 9; and Romans 8:38-39. Thus, the darkness is restrained and modified by the light. Here is where the prophetic fulfills its role and gives way to the apostolic. A brief discussion of the apostle is in order if the Lord's prophetic and the apostolic moves are to successfully fuse.

The Apostolic—God's Earthly Principalic Stronghold

John 1–2 tells us the prophet foreruns the apostle. The apostle is the human investment of God's principalic powers and their dispensations. One of the two most important synonyms for the word *apostle* is the term *principalia* for our word *principality*. The second one is *plenipotentiary*.

The terms collectively show the scope of apostolic authority in God's worlds and reveal the weight of responsibility Christ puts upon them as officers. It is Jesus Christ's direct summons and commissioning of apostles that make them His principalities on earth in their respective sub-realms and spheres. In this do they exhibit and exercise the omnipotence and sovereign power of God the Father as given to the Son of Man.

Before the apostle can do this, however, he or she must have the way of their ministry prepared for them by the prophet. This is what John the Baptist did, as told by Luke in his early chapters. Luke stated that a prophet on the order of Elijah would come and turn the hearts of the fathers to the children, and the children to the fathers. Essentially John's goal was to prepare the people to receive and participate in the next phase of the Lord's plan. As forerunner, his task was to clear the heart path of the debris, fallout, and calamities the people had grown accustomed to living with every day. John foreran Jesus, as was foretold, preaching the word of repentance, and baptizing with water to foreshadow the Lord's baptism with the Holy Spirit. When John effectively recognized and confirmed Christ as the Messiah, the focus of activity shifted from him to Jesus.

How Prophetic Movements Begin

Prophets usually start their movements with cries for repentance. They invoke the people of God to renounce their sins and abandon their secular and humanist contests with the Most High and holy God. Elijah's Mount Carmel contest was no more than this. Prophets do this to promote people's readiness for the coming of the apostle.

Prelude to Apostleship

When once the truth and righteousness power beams of God have been reinstalled, the ground is now ready for the apostle to come forward with the next phase of God's plans. Here is where previous moves that limned the upcoming apostolic move take shape. Prophets begin the arduous interpretive process of linking the now word of God to its preceding move to propel saints forward into what God wants to set in motion. The mold is sculpted for the architecture of what the Lord will do next. The apostle then takes up his or her place as the present generation's principalic stronghold of the Lord Jesus Christ in human form. Ideally, the two team up and take the next leg of the ministry's journey onward in the race.

The apostle's house (the church, its affiliates, and intra-extra ministries along with its congregation) then serve God as a territorial stronghold. They furthermore become a supernatural watch station for the Lord, one of His jurisdictional precincts. It is where His territorial angels (similar to those over the seven churches in Revelation) are assigned and serve. Now you can see what the opening words of the Lord's revelation to the seven churches are indicating. The superintendent of that spiritual precinct, the church, is the church prophet. The pastor functions as its governor when the church is not answering to an apostle. In this context, the pastor is over the prophet. If there is a bishop over the church, or an apostle, the pastor fills his or her role beneath them.

Ministry Under Apostleship

The apostle or bishop licenses pastoral performance, which is nevertheless still above the church prophet. The bulk of the church's spiritual weight and authority is *delegated*, according to God, to the prophet of the church by the prophet. God's ideal however is that the two, the pastor and the prophet, form a bond that makes delineation of each one's authority and roles incidental and not paramount.

Chapter 6

Church Prophet's Role

How the Church Prophets Differ from Itinerants

To understand the church prophet's role, we start by giving some fundamentals on the position. Our goal is to validate church or resident prophets and help define their role in the church. Of course, for us the best place to begin is in the scriptures. The following material comes from an extensive study of Hosea 12:13. The passage reads, "By a prophet the Lord brought Israel out of Egypt, and by a prophet he was preserved." The relevance of this teaching centers on the two words used to describe what Moses the prophet did, and continued to do, in the life of the people God had him deliver from bondage. Implications behind Israel's exodus and Moses' subsequent guardianship over the delivered people of God shed light on the constant work of the prophet following deliverance. Its inclusion in Hosea's discourses insights us further, beyond what we learned about Samuel's ministry on how the prophet may be utilized in the local church. From their meanings, it may be deduced that every church needs a prophetic guard. This is the primary and standing purpose of the church prophet. Without one, the church is vulnerable to humanist and demonic victimization and can easily lapse into their original bondage.

Two words used in this passage show what ancient prophets did. Together they enlighten us on the functions of stationary prophets in today's church. Jointly they give a sketch of the work these officers are to do in the modern church. The two words are *alah* and *shamar*. We concentrate on, in this discussion, the Hebrew word *shamar*. It means to "guard." Regarding the prophet, these definitions are a good guide for those who cover our churches with their prophetic mantles and mandates in the 21st century. *Shamar* clarifies their functional activities and responsibilities in local congregations.

God's Plan for the Church Prophet

The church prophet, as God intended, is to watch, guard, protect, fence in, patrol (heavenly realms), war, pray, and intercede for their assigned churches. This responsibility includes their constant purview of Christian doctrinal and theological outpourings in their generations. Church prophets should not conduct their offices in a vacuum. They should be aware of new teachings and movements taking place around them so they can endorse or renounce them. In this they spiritually and supernaturally guard the Lord's church as long as it is on earth. Our description of the ministry of the contemporary prophet as taken from the book of Hosea involves the prophetic in all of these because of *shamar*'s meaning, as defined below.

Shamar Prophetics

The word *shamar* means "to keep and guard safely; to preserve and protect." Think about this prophetically to see how one so assigned achieves these in the church.

The church as a spiritual entity on earth enjoys the bulk of what is performed or accomplished for it in the realm of the spirit. Its officiations, as executed by the prophet, use mostly supernatural means. Prayer

vigils and intercessions, spiritual warfare, divine revelations, interpretation, and translation of the old to the new are either performed or main-
tained for the local congregation by the prophet assigned to it. At first
glance, they seem pitiable and insignificant in comparison to human initiatives because of their essentially spiritual contexts and nature. Further
study reveals an inherent potency in these methods to earthly blessings
that make any carnal or humanist tactic feeble in contrast.

Hence, local church prophets, above all, should endeavor to attend
prayer sessions held by the church. How else can revelations imparted to
prayer groups be balanced and validated by a credible witness? Also, in
no other way, outside actual participation in the congregation's prayer
vigils, can church prophets effectively and intelligently battle darkness
for the flock. Prophet's spirits are powerful and so easily release blessings
and victories to the church that may otherwise be held up by demons.
Their respected presence successfully guards and keeps the territory given
by God to a particular church body. A church prophet who does not
participate in a congregation's corporate prayer life regularly is a guard
disconnected with his or her purpose for being on the wall, or unenlight-
ened on the mien of prophetic ministry.

Church prophets are to further participate in, and spiritually see to,
the officiations of church sacraments and special ceremonies such as weddings, christenings, and baptisms. In this capacity, the church prophet is
on hand with a ready word from the Lord on the event being celebrated.
Likewise, their presence immediately preserves the protocols, practices,
and executions of the services and keeps God's aims at the heart of it. As
the supernatural agent of the Godhead in attendance, they ward off un-
godliness, error, abuse, and neglect when competently trained.

General Church Prophet Tasks

Churches and their leadership should be well versed on where and how
to employ their church prophets. For instance, one case in point is at the

christening of new babies. All new babes born into the world have a divine purpose, which can be revealed to the parents by God's prophets. The church prophet's role then, is to divulge that purpose to the parents before negative world influences have a chance to subvert or inseminate the child's destiny. Ideally, parents will use the prophet's revelation to nurture the youngster in God's divine purpose. Children in the church should have ample time to hear from God about their lives as much as the adults. Having trained prophets minister to them to give them practice is a good developmental exercise; likewise, with the new convert, or the one newly baptized in Jesus. Church prophets should be in attendance when or soon after their conversions or baptism to minister the Lord's word on their new life and to cover them with the mantle of the church. The way they were nurtured naturally may attempt to overthrow the will of God in their life, so the Lord's higher powers must intervene early to prevent needless upsets and diversions that take them off course. The revelations of the church prophet can place the newcomer to Christ on his or her destiny path and settle them in their New Creation destiny.

Church membership too can benefit from this resident ministry from time to time. If church members were able to hear from the Lord prophetically in their home church regularly under the auspices of their pastor, then fewer saints would be seduced to follow questionable prophets' ministries, or resort to psychics to hear about their futures. Another important function of the prophet is prophetic counsel. This embraces more than prophesying; it is advisory prophetics that blends present insight, future wisdom, and divine revelation.

Beyond this, the church prophet should be part of the clergy representatives in membership crises like death, illness, calamity, and so forth. It is the prophet's word that assures the demons involved in the attack are halted and do not tread past their assigned or permitted bounds. Read over David's penalty for counting Israel and how the Lord told the angel on assignment in the judgment when to draw back his sword. The ac-

count is in 1 Chronicles 21. Another good activity for the church prophet
is being with the church's members who have to face and interact with
world authorities like judges, police, and so forth. The respectful presence of the church prophet interceding in the background and uphold-
ing the will and word of the Lord in the matter could soothe otherwise
explosive situations. And above all else, the church prophet should be
present and involved at the church's major outreach functions, and it
goes without saying that the mature ones should be collaborators on the
church's business matters. If you read 1 Kings 22:6–13; Ezra 5:1; and
Nehemiah 6:7, how this all works becomes clearer.

Avoid Prophetic Monopolies

It should be said here, in conclusion, that the church prophet institution
should not be limited to just one prophet. The one chosen to *superintend*
the ministry of the local church should be free to identify, nurture, and
induct others into the ministry to help shoulder the workload. Also, having more than one prophet reduces the possibility of prophetic monopoly
in the church and allows the membership to hear from God in more than
one dimension.

Pastors should seek to establish the ministry of the church prophet as
an ordained order that includes prophetic representation from all the
relevant spheres of the church's life.

The Watchman Duties of the Church Prophet

Going back to the word *shamar* that we have been discussing, it further
means "to watch over as one who is a guard over cattle or sheep. It applies
to a prophet." Sheep in this case is referring to the flock of a congregation. In the church it means church members. Many of you already know
that another word for the prophet is *watchman*. Its use symbolizes the
patrolling and guardianship activities of the officer in the supernatural
realm. Thus, the watch center of the church prophet's territory coincides

with their church's divinely appointed sphere.

Watchman duties then are accomplished through the prayer, intercessions, and petitions of the prophet on behalf of the church. They comprise the many reasons a prophet should be installed as the superintendent of the church's overall *prophetics,* and head of its spiritual guard, particularly over the prayer group. Such a guard would consist of the prayer team, the special intercessors, dedicated psalmists, seers, and of course subordinate prophets. The *watchman* application spotlights links between what prophets do spiritually and what a similar officer would do in the natural realm. Thus, the word *shamar* emphatically gives prophets the status of spiritual guards, warriors, supernatural enforcers, and keepers of the churches of God. See Jeremiah 17:16 and 50:6–7 as examples.

Additionally, our word *shamar* identifies a prophet who encircles (or surrounds) to retain and attend to, as one does a garden. The prophet's spiritual authority acts as a fence or garrison around an assigned congregation to shield it from harm, attack, or demonic trespass. Protection from trespassers, as meant here, includes protection from the spoilage, destruction, invasion, and threats that result from spiritual and human trespassers in the church. There are times heretical types or wayward renegades join a church just to sow seeds of destruction in it. The watchful eye of the resident prophet can spot these people and bring spiritual discomfort to bear on them so they are ill at ease among the flock and quickly leave. This tactic is always engaged by occultists in the church's neighborhood.

On the other hand, in the congregations where the prophetic is refused, the same situation can have disastrous results. By the time church leaders become aware of the sly manipulations of roaming renegades, it is often too late. Usually excessive generosity, overt assistance, and frequent volunteering at the outset obscure their tactics. Therefore, the ulterior motive that brought them to the church is submerged beneath a veneer of good deeds—charity work. Witches and other destructive occultists rely on this tactic to infiltrate and contaminate the churches they target for attack. Months, years, even decades can go by before the scheme is uncovered without a discerning and well-respected prophetic eye. In the meantime, countless souls could have been lost to the church because of the free course given a saboteur of darkness.

For an additional example of the detriment of a prophetic void, see the effect of Elisha's death on Israel in the book of 2 Kings 13:14–21. The account gives a biblical picture of how the absence of the prophet is used advantageously by the enemy. Notice how the band of raiders attempting to invade the area was successful only after his death. The *spiritual void,* better yet *prophetic void,* left by Elisha's demise enabled their attack on the land to finally succeed.

Shamar Upheld by Kindred Term

Our *shamar* teaching is supported by a kindred term that validates its truth. It is the word *natsar,* and legitimizes the watchman status of the prophet in the contemporary church by expanding previous church prophet responsibilities.

The resident or staff prophet is to spiritually and practically engage in activities that protect, preserve, maintain, observe the quality of the church, its basis for existing, its stability, and its congregant growth. He or she is obliged to observe and spiritually nurture its communal life. This even includes inspecting their worship and recreational forms, educational doctrines, and kingdom practices to see they are consistent with scripture and compatible with the nature of the Godhead in conduct, perspective, and manifestation.

Natsar prophetic functions surround the church as one does a well-guarded city. That makes the prophetic guard a human wall about the church and a spiritual shield by which the Lord hides the congregation from attack. The prophet's covenanted spiritual authority intervenes for the church as the mantle cloaks it to conceal its vulnerabilities. In this way, the stationed church prophet fortifies the church he or she covers as a cultivating fortress in God's high places. In this capacity, the prophet protects the house from the bondage and strongholds of idolatry, spiritual intimidation, and ecumenical compromise. They spot even secular holds and humanist philosophy lurking in traditional church doctrines unknown to most. See Jeremiah 4:16 for an expanded understanding of God's mind on this duty, which is also what Nahum 2:1 is talking about.

By the preceding discussions, you can see that prophets are fighters. It is the nature of the mantle and the requirement of the task. They must be fearless, determined, resolute, and protective. If not, they are mere newscasters that announce what is going on with no godly effect on the events happening in the church whatsoever. Obviously, character and temperament like this can be harmful without divine restraint. That is why prophets must be painstakingly obedient and fiercely loyal to the Lord. However hurtful the job may be at times, the prophet is dangerous if they have not surrendered their hurts and disappointments to the Lord. Those that do not turn to the Lord risk raiding, intentionally or not, His treasures. Then the prophet ceases to be a servant and frightfully becomes a supernatural mercenary using powerful abilities to finance their whims or reward themselves for all they suffered. Read God's answer to this prophetic attitude in Micah 3:5.

Pastors, in light of this information, ask yourself if you could use some added spiritual help and increased supernatural covering for those entrusted to your care. If so, you are an ideal candidate for a church or resident prophet.

In the next chapter, I present information to guide shepherds and church prophets in their discovery and installation of this ministry. Also outlined are more valuable uses of the church prophet in a local church.

Chapter 7

CHURCH PROPHET

Contemporary Application of Ancient Guide

Previously you were introduced to the validity of the church prophet in the local church. The office and officer were discussed from the perspective of Hosea 12:13 and the Hebrew words *shamar* and *natsar.* Here we pick up the study from that point.

From what you read previously about the *shamar* function of the prophet, you now understand how the church prophet is to fulfill spiritual and practical functions. It can be said, for comparison's sake, their *watch care* functions closely resemble that of resident watchers in certain secular institutions, for example, in fraternity houses, sororities, rehabilitation houses, and similar institutions where personnel are assigned to oversee, tend to, and safeguard resident. Any overseer of communal dwelling or gathering place whose position is more than custodial, to use an earthly example, fits this category. Observing the functional preoccupations of such custodial care superintendents clearly illustrates this aspect of the church prophet's spiritual purpose.

All Important Church Prophet Requisite—Submission

In the church house, a prophet's authority is subject to the pastor for the duration of the assignment. The reason for this is simple. The church and its members were given to the shepherd, and not the prophet. Read Gad's and Nathan's service under David's reign for how this works.

Resident Prophet Church and Leader Interaction

Nathan and Gad were *nabi* prophets to the king, although Gad was a seer. They served as resident or stationary prophets, as discussed earlier in the book. Nonetheless, their presence, assignment, or spiritual authority as staff prophets did not negate David's regency over the land. Although their word had great power and induced the supernatural, their positions did not subjugate or supersede David's reign. The two royal officers served him as counselors, seers, intercessors, sages, and prophetic warriors with authorized voices in the supernatural. Their greatest contribution was their official license to invoke the nation's potent spiritual powers and responses in this world. If you read Deuteronomy 32:9–13, you see that the Lord established Israel in a spherical as well as natural high place. Covenantal relationship with the Most High God brings with it the benefit of abiding in His highest realms. David understood this, as may be seen from reading his words in 2 Samuel 22:34. He saw those of his cabinet as spiritual high powers assigned to his reign, as they were with Saul.

When Saul and Jonathan were slain, David understood that they had fallen from their high places and their deaths were a most likely consequence of their weakening. Job 25:2 fortifies this truth by declaring the Lord makes peace (indicating His sovereign authority) in His high places. Read with this Psalm 18:33. For future teaching on the subject so it makes more sense to you, think about "God's highest places" reference in this light. Psalm 18:33; Isaiah 14:14; 2 Samuel 22:34; and Habakkuk 3:19. They all share the same idea of what is meant. Prophets need to grasp this concept since they are the physical embodiment of God's high place representatives in their churches.

Spiritually, such high place references, rendered by the Hebrew word *bamah,* define the clouds and the highest waves of the seas. It speaks to the heavenly and celestial spheres of God as much as it refers to the high powers of the earth and their corresponding authority.

His prophets' spiritual high places effected their positions of authority with David. Their mantles gave the king direct and immediate access to the spontaneous will and word of the Lord on routine and unexpected matters. For this function to be fruitful, it is obvious that prayer must be a great part of the watch duties of the prophet who serves a church.

Remember, intercession and prayer, not merely prophesying, are priority jobs of the prophet. Without a stringent and potent prayer life, church prophets would rely on their *soulish realm* for revelation. They could then risk prophesying out of their own hearts (Jeremiah 23:16) or their own spirits (Ezekiel 13:1–3). That is defined as divination, discussed later. The perceptions of the leader and the whims of the flock can prevail in these cases more than anything else. Worse than that is the church prophet who fails to read the scriptures regularly or seek the Lord for the prophetic ministrations. Here Jeremiah 23:13 is the outcome. The spiritual principles and laws of creation see to that, because what is written in Isaiah 66:4 and Jeremiah 23:13 can be the only consequence.

Church Prophet Lifestyle and Posture of the Church

Prayer, separation from the world, and devotion to God are the phase one acts of prophetic preparation. After these, a rigid adherence to the Spirit and word of God alone assures church prophets consistently deliver the pure words of the Lord to those in their care. Neglecting such requisites and constant fraternizing with the household are the greatest dangers to prophets' accuracy. Here is why.

Excessive mingling with those he or she serves can cause prophets' devotion to their charge to overrule the will of the Lord in certain situations. Hearing too often their problems, needs, and plights firsthand can so arouse the prophet's compassion or opinions that he or she can confirm what the Lord may not have ordained. The incident of King David's desire to build a house for God in the book of 2 Samuel 7:1–29 makes this point.

As you can read from the account, Nathan the prophet's constant interactions with David caused him to give David a word from the sphere of the obvious. He prophesied the obviously predictable when asked by David if he thought God would be pleased if the king built Him a house in which to dwell. Nathan told David to go on and build God a house, because his experience with the king had shown him how pleased Jehovah was with him. In the prophet's mind, God's good pleasure was so abundantly evident in the king's life that the Lord could not possibly deny David the honor of building him a temple. After the prophet gave God's consent to the king, he was later sent to reverse his word following a vision given him in the night. It is a good thing Nathan the prophet was not too proud to reverse his word with the king and give the real word of the Lord on the matter. Many prophets today would not do so for fear of professional embarrassment or being labeled a false prophet.

Instead of allowing the king's sacrifice to be spurned by God and his time, money, and energy to be wasted on what would not have pleased the Lord, Nathan boldly gave the king what he learned was the true mind of God on his plans. In this case, revelation could have been jeopardized by familiarity and both could have been dangerous. Thanks to the humility of the prophet it was not. His willingness to admit his mistake meant the king's desire was denied for hallowed reasons only. Due to David's military career, which involved much bloodshed on God's behalf, building a house for the Lord was assigned to one of his sons, Solomon.

This example shows that for the church prophet in particular, the line between friendship and familiarity can easily grow thin and fade. Warm feelings and fortified trust that grow between the prophet and the pastor could eliminate boundaries and relax standards to the point where the prophet's mantle in the church becomes merely a spiritual prop. It can also be the other way around. The pastor's authority in the union gets so weakened that the prophet disregards it in favor of what he or she is certain the Lord is saying.

When familiarity takes hold, the pastor can claim to have a church prophet but over time nullify the messenger's value to the church and its leaders. I have been in such situations in the past. When indicated, the decision to dissolve treasured relationships or withdraw from comfortable fellowships for professional reasons was difficult. Being aware of the gravity of my office and the conditions under which such relationships were formed, I recognize when God's motivation for my being in someone's life was being jeopardized. I not only distance myself when familiarity begins to border on contempt, but I do so for the benefit of the person greatly in need of God's prophetics. It is quite easy for prophets to get to the place that they commune with someone so much the person forgets who they are and are meant to be in their life.

At these times, joint prayer sessions yield little objectivity and the prophet begins to sit on important information received from God. He or she starts to question the veracity of the words prophetics receive because of being too close to the situation at hand. Or the prophet worries about threatening the friendship if they give their pastor-friend a word they will not like. As the days go by, the prophet grows more timid by the friendship, fearing pastoral reprisal and retaliation. Wisdom dictates under these circumstances that the problem is brought out into the open and frankly discussed. If the suspicions of the prophet are true and their usefulness to the pastor is finished, then good decisions should be made as the two accept that the prophet's time with the ministry is up. For sure this can prove painful, but it is prudent. Responsible plans should be made to make the transition from the old to the new prophet as smooth as possible.

Even with this inevitable likelihood, which need not be viewed with negativity, God still would like to provide His Davids of today with the same benefit as their ancient predecessor by installing like prophets in all His churches. Truly the church needs a solid, competent, masterful *nabiim* institution today operating in His integrity. The Lord yearns to give His pastors the advantage they need over darkness by assigning a potent *spiritual watchforce* to guard and defend His churches from their onslaughts.

As operatives of the divine kingdom of the Most High, prophets spiritual authority in the church's realm should easily supersede that of the kingdom of darkness. Not restricted to the supernatural alone, the church prophet's activities that effectively impact the spirit world can effortlessly overcome the edicts of human kingdoms as well, another value they bring to the church. According to the scriptures, the prophets of God should *profit* those they serve, not merely themselves. Their mature presence in a land says that prosperity on all fronts should be at the church's disposal over time.

The Benefit of Voluntary Church Prophet Submission to the Church

While it is true the prophet is the second ranking Ephesians 4:11 official, those assigned to local churches voluntarily submit to the shepherd to cooperate with the will and purposes of God. Their decisions to do so allow them to effectively collaborate with the head of the church on matters pertaining to the Lord and the church, and enables all concerned to yield the peaceable fruit of obedience. These prophets take care not to usurp the pastor or attempt to draw away the sheep as disciples after themselves. They shun the very appearance of these behaviors before the membership, deliberately giving the pastor due regard in every public instance. From their hearts they know they are in the church on divine assignment and their job is to uphold the pastor in every credible way. In addition, submitted church prophets see to it the sheep do not see them as alternatives to the pastor and attempt to pit the two (the prophet and the pastor) against each other. Church prophets do not shepherd the sheep they cover and guard outside the pastor; they protect and develop them in the Lord's spirituality.

I once had a prophet of a church whose agenda was wholly dichotomous to mine. I called a meeting with this novice to try to get to the bottom of a similar problem. I thought that if I discussed the matter with him personally, he would see the value of a functioning collaboration between us. It did not work. You see, as long as the prophet was free to lead, prophesy, and perform, everything was fine. When I imposed boundaries and guidelines on him, his attitude turned sullen.

In the meeting, the young prophet became belligerent and informed me that he was not giving his life to ministry; he had a life outside of it and he would not permit me to tell him what to do. Taken aback a bit, I let him know that the two perspectives were mutually exclusive of the prophet's office. His life was no longer his own and a church prophet assignment like a mentorship presupposed his being told what to do. The words had no effect. The prophet countered by adding that he would determine when he would or would not obey me. I was stunned, as I had never imagined these disorders brewing in this person's belief system. They had come to me from under a reputable and well-known prophet and I assumed the person had these basics of the prophetic resolved. They did not.

After a few more, "I'm grown and don't need anyone to tell me what to do and where I can go" tantrums, the prophet informed me that he had to seek God on my request. I had asked that he give me advance notice when he would be leaving town or not make a service and that was his response. Naturally, I saw the entire arrangement had grown dysfunctional and said as much. My answer to our young prophet was that any position with any organization would require such notification and that the issue at hand was not a matter of adulthood or childhood. It was a matter of accountability—professional accountability. I realized that this young prophet would be embarking on a long road to learn two very primitive prophet lessons: obedience and accountability. If it were not for the insight into what the Lord was going to have to do to teach him that the two go hand in hand, and that one cannot be without the other, I would have been more disturbed. As it was, I grieved sort of like Samuel over Saul because knowing God, I saw that it was going to get rough for this young learner.

Rather than wait for the prophet to pray and get God's answer, I severed the relationship by releasing the novice from my tutelage. I knew this outburst masked deep-rooted problems springing from other issues that hindered his ability to grasp elementary prophetic principles. Cases like these show why church prophets should not be installed who have problems with accountability, reporting to the pastor as instructed or performing their duties according to the pastor's directives. These all amount to insubordination and will culminate in a church insurrection. After a while that is what happened in my case. The young prophet, convinced he was ready to go it alone, gathered a number of other neophytes and began to teach them. Ironically, the very obedience they required of their new followers is wanting in themselves. I am sure many pastors have been in this place, and the sagest answer I can give you is to cut ties early, quickly, decisively, and avoid infecting the rest of your germinating leaders should a prophet be unwilling to listen and learn from you.

I am reminded at this point of those churches whose staff prophets have diverted the flock's attention from the pastor to themselves. In some instances, the act of treason was so great that even the tithes due the church were diverted to the prophet. I have experienced this myself. A prophet, afraid he will not get the opportunity to do his ministry, attaches himself to a church for one reason, which is to ingratiate himself to the pastor long enough to seduce the spiritually hungry or immature members with his prophetics. Once the prophet's ministry has dazzled the susceptible members of the church, the prophet creates a situation where he can retaliate against the pastor for an artificial hurt by abruptly leaving the church, freeing himself to launch his ministry with his or her flock. Beckoning disgruntled members they have inflamed over time, the prophet sets up a ministry to rival the church and convince its membership to support their work. They instruct them to bring their tithes to the prophet's meetings to finance their rebellion. This is error, as the scripture records no prophet's authorized to receive congregational tithes and offerings due the church they serve, or to splinter a church down prophetic lines. It should be underscored here that tithes generally go to the priests (shepherds) of the household and not to the church or itinerant prophet. To do otherwise could have a congregant's giving go unrecognized by God.

Prophets receive, and are entitled to, offerings and support for their labors, but not the tithes from the church to which they have been assigned without the pastor's approval. Prophets truly sent by God will encourage congregants to surrender their tithes to the church and not to themselves for obedience' sake. They will also urge church members to remain under the covering of their pastors and not seek prophetic experiences in their place outside the church. You will know a God-groomed prophet by the fact that if they leave, they will do so quietly, informing the pastor and refusing to incite other members or leaders to leave with them.

How Church Prophets Are Financed

A staff prophet should be compensated regularly like any other permanent or long-term employee if they are to forego traveling ministry to serve one church. If not, the danger of their abandoning their posts to provide for themselves is great and this endangers both the church and its head unnecessarily. As soon as it is practical, the staff prophet should be routinely compensated like any other employee of the church or work. It cannot be stressed enough that if you require your prophet to remain in the church, you must compensate them sufficiently to do so. Such compensation need not totally come directly or exclusively out of the church budget and may be only partly allocated from church income. But you should allow your staff prophet to hold prophetic meetings, seminars, classes, and such under the church's auspices where they can attract offerings. The cost of such meetings should be borne by the prophets themselves with fees assessed according to what their personal ministry can afford. The prophet should also as well tithe from the money they raised from the church's covering. Under these conditions, it is helpful to urge the membership to pledge to support the local church's prophetic institution.

Standard Position of the Church Prophet

When one serves as a church prophet, he or she stands watch in the realm of the spirit over the pastor and the church for their good. They are not to become occupied with the church's demise or destruction. Should the church be involved in something dangerous, God expects the church prophet to pray and intercede for it to turn its heart and soul back to the Lord. Here is one more reason novice prophets should not be installed as church prophets. I have found that young and untrained prophetic people see only evil and doom in the beginning of their ministries. They discern who will die and what God should judge more than anything else. The fundamental nature of prophetic character inspires it until divine nurturing teaches them otherwise. An early predisposition to the flesh can motivate newcomers to the prophetic to confuse their soulish realm with the Spirit of God. Consequently, what they hear from God, although it comes pure, mixes with their immaturity, hurts, and anger, making them mistakenly deliver opinions, perspectives, and perceptions as prophecy. The tendency risks their being more psychic then prophetic. It does not mean they are serving occultism, but that they are more attuned to the intelligence of their soul than the revelations of the Spirit initially.

We have had new or unrefined prophets in our prayer groups and identified their immaturity and instability in the after-prayer visions and words they received. I remember remarking about one such seer that they only received negative words and visions from the Lord. It did not matter who the subject was; the word and revelations they received were consistently destructive. The seer's natural negative personality had yet to be purged and so their hope for anything they viewed as wrong in the Lord was that He would shut it down and/or destroy the work. It is not uncommon for people who have been abused or dominated by overbearing authority figures in their lives to see the only resolution of insurmountable problems as destruction and death. Therefore, when they come to God, they are immediately enraptured with His power to destroy all wrong and annihilate wrongdoers. Years of frustration and futility have bred in them the need for God to avenge them, even if the offense is merely being forced to witness a shortfall in another. These prophets early years are fraught with the four D's of damnation: doom, death, disease, and destruction. The redemptive and nurturing elements of the office come later. It takes awhile for them to see this as apparent misuse of their supernatural faculties and an outright imposition of their personal criticism on the Spirit of God.

Seasoned prophetic servants on the other hands are on guard for potential harm and danger lurking to invade their flocks. Mature prophets recognize them as man-made tools of enlightenment such as mysticism, occultism, secularism, humanism, and that most insidious seducer, tradition. Prophets of the church are to recognize the signs and symptoms of their invaders and combat them successfully while doing their best to keep the work intact and moving forward in God. They do not see their presence or infiltration as grounds for the destruction of the work as the novice prophet does. Education and training are how prophets avoid this however, and so your church prophet must be learned in these and other prophetic subjects to expose them to the tricks the devil uses to get them to *prophesy* his will on the churches. You will know these groups by their death to the church campaigns, and any injured prophet can fall into the trap. They are always comparing notes of doom and are unwilling for the Lord to forgive and redeem His works. They remind you of Jonah the prophet in his Ninevah disappointment.

When God wanted to forgive and spare the land, the prophet became angry and pouted because he wanted God's judgment to fall on it. To reiterate, preventing this attitude calls for education and training. Without it, the untrained and slightly educated church prophet, stunted in ministry revelation and prophetic reach, tends to be doom-and-gloom minded. Such a minister can end up being no more than a megaphone in the congregation, amplifying doom's voice, or a busybody in the church's affairs, not impacting its people positively or appreciably.

Later we discuss the necessary insights, abilities, and training a church prophet should have. Highest of them is compassion for the flock. Church prophets are injurious if they are unmoved by the weaknesses of the flock, of those who are not granted their degree of wisdom and spiritual fortitude. I have seen some of them so intent on being right that they are contemptuous of the sheep's suffering. It is good that all prophets remain objective and responsibly detached, especially those of the local church. However, these professional safeguards should not overshadow basic Christian compassion.

Chapter 8

Your Church
Prophet

Church Prophet Institution—Local Church Prophetics

Prophetics in the local church operate very differently from the free flow motions of the itinerant prophet. The fluidity of the prophetic has a difficult molding to the necessary institutions of the church. Of all the reasons for this, the chief one is that the church prophet comes under the pastor, and that restricts the normal authority and latitude they enjoy. When it comes to the local church prophet, the assignment is not unlike the one between a contracted, howbeit respected advisor and his or her serving organization. If the prophet has not been broken and pruned by God, the arrangement could prove disastrous as the mainly ethereal mantle of the prophet clashes with the nurturing one pastors wear.

Potential conflicts notwithstanding, there is much value to the arrangement. For it to work, prophets serving in a church must be aware that they are voluntarily for the good of the gospel surrendering great portions of their ordinary authority and privileges to fulfill another's mission and mandate. The decision is not unlike Christ when He came to earth to carry out the Father's mission according to Philippians 2:7. He deliberately made Himself of no reputation, knowing that what He was before the assignment became irrelevant to the task at hand.

When a prophet comes into a local church because God has assigned him or her there, the object of their sojourn is to carry out what the Lord wants the church to do. The challenge comes in when prophets find it hard to do so without disrupting the church's culture and operations, or when they must discredit its present headship to succeed. The Lord expects the prophet to meld with the church's leadership and integrate his or her mantle in the customary life of the work as a support. Whatever authority the prophet on local church assignment wields is subject to that of the existing government of the church for the duration of the charge. And charge is a good word here, because it includes the personal and professional cost of the duty, as well as the cost of its breadth of responsibility.

Prophets are errant (and arrant) if they see their call as one sent to wrest the sheep from under the pastor's covering. When one meets a prophet who is extracting sheep from the church from which they came and presuming to draw them unto themselves, this is a prophet that is going against divine order. I recently had someone say that they were leaving their church because a beloved friend intruded into the office of the prophet. I say intruded because if the prophet were genuine and not a novice, they would be of a mind to spare the flock and therefore would discourage their friend from leaving pastoral covering to personally serve their new calling. The reason the member gave for selecting their friend's position over their pastor is that they viewed their friend as their *personal* prophet. What a dangerous mentality. No one is meant to have a *personal* prophet to the exclusion of the rest of the body of Christ, and no prophet is ordained to strictly serve any individual or small isolated clique's will. Proverbs 18:1 says why, while Judges 17:1 gives us such an example in the Bible of this practice's detriment. When you read the account, you learn that only an idolatrous heart devoid of leadership resorts to such a spiritual order.

In the account, a man named Micah robbed his mother for his own objectives. He did not tell her he took her money and she subsequently reacted by putting a curse on the thief. When he realized that his mother's curse could affect him, he confessed his crime and she negated her curse. In a bizarre turn of events, she gave him part of the money back to fulfill his heart's desire to craft himself an idol. After he had done so, he invented an ancestral religion where he installed his own priests. Of course, we know that during that era, fathers were considered the head of their houses and so the authority to do so rested in Micah. However, this was not a pagan family but an Israelite one and that exacerbated the situation.

Meanwhile, a Levite (minister) was preparing to launch out on his own. Seeking a place to dwell, and presumably to offer his services, he happened upon Micah the idolater. The two men forged a covenant whereby the Levite would be the priest and officiate over Micah's new family religion. Judges 17:6 explains how Israel's spirituality became so deteriorated. There was no kingship, headship, and so the people did whatever came into their hearts and minds. The Levite was supported by the idolater and lost sight of his initial calling. He ended up staying with Micah the idolater to serve as his personal priest. Read the last verse of the account.

God discourages prophets from seeing themselves as envoys of individuals, instead of envoys of the cause of Christ dispatched to His church. When the cause of Christ is intended, then keeping sheep in their churches and serving the wider body of Christ become the prophet's primary objectives. If not, then it is safe to mark such a prophet as a wayward usurper of divine authority and shun their divisive spirit.

I have had many conversations with prophets rising to the call from within a local church where they may have often spent years. Suddenly, they legitimately sense the call to the office of the prophet. What happens next determines their credibility and God's long-term use of them in His service. Sadly, a great percentage of them respond to God's awakening crudely. They awkwardly manifest their gifts, abruptly sever ties, and callously crush loving pastor's hearts. In naïve zeal they recklessly disrupt the flow of the church where they grew in the Lord so badly that they must be excommunicated.

Other cases are that some emerging prophets foster division by exercising their newfound ministries outside the confines of the church, refusing to be supervised by the pastors they now feel are beneath them. A distasteful struggle begins that can fragment the loyalties of the membership and wound many vulnerable sheep. Both extremes are infectious and should be curtailed.

I remember talking to one prophet of a church who started a prophetic school, outside of the church and declined to submit it to the pastor, even though the lion's share of their students came from the sizeable congregation. As if that were not damaging enough, the prophet shunned significant service in the church. They avoided prayer, never established a serviceable prophetic institute, and failed to identify and participate in grooming arising prophets in the church. Instead there was nothing but chaos in the church as a prophetic void was created by the prophet's disobedience. That disobedience released its seeds to flourish throughout the body contaminating the faith of many.

On the Positive Side

Of course, there are always two sides to every conflict and the above is no different. On too many occasions, prophets are suffocated in their churches by overprotective pastors who mean well but nonetheless sacrifice their prophetics to protect the flock. This regularly happens before the prophet has an opportunity to disrupt or subvert the work at all. Reacting to far too many horror stories and very little knowledge, normally tender and open-minded pastors can unintentionally slaughter a beginning prophet out of fear and overlook more positive options.

One positive option is to nurture the young prophet and seek to establish the bounds of their ministry and its service requirements for your church (i.e. training, probationary trial, apprenticeship, mentoring, and the like). Test the prophets' intentions by assigning them an important yet noncritical sphere of the ministry to manage and prophetically cultivate. If the person remains within the confines of the agreement, then you can increase their reach in the body and their weight of responsibility. This process should take two to three years if the prophet is new. If the novice completes the process you can move forward or identify quality prophetic education to which to refer them. Also, you do not have to wait two or three years for their formal education and training to commence. The two processes—your testing and their development—can go together.

Other options are seeking the wisdom of other pastors who have successfully melded the prophetic in their churches is a good way to handle yours. Turning to reputable and seasoned itinerant prophets is yet another positive step. Besides these suggestions, discuss your concerns with the budding prophets in your church honestly and objectively to elicit sound advice on how the office may be encouraged in the church. At the same time, have frank conversations with trusted colleagues about your fears to defuse tensions and enable you to take on a very important and far-reaching part of shepherding, that of nurturing, guiding, and facilitating a new officer's promotion in the Lord's kingdom. It is a great call and unfortunately too many dutiful pastors overlook or avoid it.

Boldly and competently taking on the development of the prophetic yourself not only facilitates its positive initiation in your church, but will reduce new prophets' potential to seduce your membership with mesmerizing prophetics. Be sure your new prophets understand that causing a church member to turn on its pastor is a deadly proposition, and according to Ezekiel 13:1–16 courts the Lord's wrath and costs the prophet his or her place in God's eternal assembly.

When All Options Are Exhausted

Conversely, the prophet who finds their pastor resistant to their call to the office and/or its operations, dead set against their prophetic growth and manifestation in the church will get a release from God to leave. Here is where it could get tricky. Sometimes new prophets want to exercise their ministries so badly that they believe their brief encounters with God and the few early words He gives them to say are all that is needed to get going. They are unwilling to hear about grooming, training, seasoning, and proving so they become difficult to handle. Impulsive and self-willed, they turn surly and unruly, becoming disrespectful and impudent at this stage. God has spoken to them and that makes them just as knowledgeable of His ways as those who have gone before them. Talking sense, especially God sense, to them at this point is impossible as they sit before you arrogant and defiant.

In their minds, all you (pastors) want to do is sit on their ministries. Ironically, they feel you are holding them back because you are somehow jealous of their gift or threatened by it. The leviathan spirit is all over them at this point, as they reek with pride. Read Job 41 and pay particular attention to the last few verses.

Shunning Human Instruction Courts Divine Chastening

After several attempts to reason with headstrong prophets, pastors finally conclude the best way for them to learn is the hard way. Either by mutual decision, or outright rebellion, they commit the first of their many spiritual blunders. And God's fierce pride-dissolving classes begin. Like Cain who committed a serious offense against God's divine ordinances, your young prophets too must be severed from the flock. If not, they may choose to leave to start their ministry unhindered by you—their way. Also like Cain, they are marked by the Holy Spirit as a rebel, even though they continue to be well loved by God and their pastors. Think about Mark when Paul and Barnabas traveled together. Although it took years, the young minister finally got the message and submitted to Paul after all. The unfortunate part of it was the path he took to do so. It was no doubt rough and he wasted years only to end up right where he started. It is the same way with today's hotheads.

God's invisible yet tangible mark mutes His favor on them for a time as they become fair game to the seductive and eventually brutalizing forces of darkness assigned by the Lord to facilitate their training. This spiritual analogy well considers the Lord Jesus' work on the cross which promises the young offender once trained and humbled will be restored to God's useful service. The apostle Peter well understood this from what he said in 1 Peter 5:10.

Veteran Prophets Discern Dissenters

In the meantime, seasoned prophets encountering such novices not only know these newcomers when they meet them, but discern the mark of the Lord on them. They understand why it is there. Having been that route themselves, most of them are alert to the novice's victimized tone used to explain why they are all alone against the world and the church. They hear the undertone of a stubbornness determined to carry out the prophetic their own way because everyone before them got it wrong. Moreover, mature leaders sense the independent prophet's subtle contempt for authority, resistance to accountability, and delight in assaulting the established church and its ministers.

Veterans have been there and are not easily fooled by the apparent anointing on the independent prophet's life or the amazing prophecies they utter. They learned long ago that it takes more than a high-powered gift to accredit a prophet. It takes righteousness, the love of God, maturity, and submission. Prophets above all else understand that the ministry law of God is respect for authority. Though they may be called from the ranks of the rebellious, if they are to excel in that calling, respect for authority is one reality they must prize. Jesus exemplified such respect in

Matthew 23:1–3.

Recall the staggering submission lessons they learned from God in their early years. Experienced prophets know the kingdom cannot stand without respect for authority, for its absence is the basis for the house divided. After a few moments with struggling prophets they understand the learning path the King of kings has been walking and why, and that it will make them useful to pastors who want to install church prophets in their church.

Those who have conquered what new prophets must confront and walked the well-paved road of the rebel know God's orders and are able to identify and redress those issues in others. If for no other reason than those just described, your prophetic superintendent must be comparably seasoned.

If the defiant prophet silently determines to walk away from the church, here is how to tell if they are leaving at the unction of God, or if the young prophet's flesh is reacting negatively to pastoral authority. Study the telltale signs below. Is the prophet exhibiting the following signs as they contemplate or prepare to leave? Answer the following questions to find out.

1. Did he or she show that every effort was made to serve the Lord in the church and the pastor simply rejected it? If so, then the Lord could be reassigning them.

2. Did the young prophet have a record before the conflict, of serving the church, obeying the pastor, and submitting to the church rules? If not, then their motive for leaving is most likely their own and not God's.

3. Did, or is, the young prophet leave without sowing discord among the saints and without dragging their own little following with them? Then the call to leave could be of God. Otherwise, it definitely is not.

These three factors reflect the spirit in which the prophet or any minister leaves. They can help you identify any personal ambition that may have entered and spoiled the motives of the new messenger. When this happens, know that whatever comes from such prophets' mouths can be tainted with anger or jaded with personal bias. Before resistors leave, they criticize everything, refuse to participate in anything, and leave a trail of bitterness behind.

A good rule of thumb for qualifying the prophetic motives of a potential or installed church prophet is to see how much the church at large voices their recognition of the prophet's positive influence in its vision, mission, and overall evolvement. If the prophet is not from outside the church then the church membership is the best judge of their potentiality. Good candidates for church prophet are actively involved in the membership's lives and they can attest to it. Generally speaking, the person with the most impact on the church overall appears everywhere, even if they are not in the forefront of the ministry. If a prospective church prophet is genuinely interested in the church, then their handprint will be as evident in the church's life as the pastors and other church leaders. Forefront ministers do not in themselves translate to the most effective servants. Oftentimes it is the prophetic candidate whose work is seen long before, and more than they are, that has the greatest impact.

Exploring the Church Prophet Roles

The church prophet, in addition to what has been said so far, also serves as a divinely stationed sentinel. Their prophecies sound the alarm that announces approaching danger to the pastor and the flock. A sentinel is a lookout, a demonstrator with a stake in the work they guard. They see their call as being to enclose the gaps in the church's covering. As a sentinel, the prophet of the church scouts the supernatural regions surrounding the church to spot intruders from Satan (human or spiritual) and ward off impending seductive invasions. They patrol through prayer the spiritual terrain of the ministry as God's divine watchers. Agabus performed this function for the apostles in Acts 21. Study as well Paul's final public address to the Ephesians presbytery in Acts 20:17–31. Both these examples show the sentinel work of the stationary prophet.

Furthermore, during times of carnal relapse, the church prophet is the Holy Spirit goaded objector staunchly opposing the slackening of biblically moral lines. He or she can turn agitator and resister to hold back the flows of libertinism masking itself as New Creation liberty. Invariably, church prophets whose allegiance is to God first, cast dissenting votes against anything threatening to jeopardize the church's favorable status in the eyes of the Lord. In doing so, the *nabiim* institution of the local church can rally godly supporters for the pastor's aims or blockade in prayer whatever seeks to harm, hinder, or regress the work. The very presence of church prophets can invisibly corral subtle or lurking sin and thereby close the borders of the church's sphere to protect its power link to the Almighty God. Their diligence assures the stream of priceless yet invisible treasures, coveted by darkness, are not diverted from God's people.

Prophets as God's spiritual surveillance networks watch the landscape of the supernatural to report on and prevent demonic breakthroughs in their protective fences from occurring. They do on earth what the heavenly watchers of Daniel 4:23 and Zechariah 1:10 and 5:7 do in the spirit. Actually, the heavenly watcher reveals what the church prophet must know to defend his or her post, as mature prophets interact with God's angels. Therefore, every prophet's mantle is awakened by these supernatural counterparts. And all bona fide prophets, without exception, are initiated by interactions with these powerful agents of God's invisible creation. No prophet can be genuine without an irrepressible awareness of the spiritual guard that surrounds them that supernaturally sees to God's work and will on earth. The prophet's presence on its own validates the minister as he or she unavoidably speaks in all God's worlds as casually as the one in which we dwell. Consequently, church or staff prophets should be perceptive enough to detect invader's steal in their flock and discern the good from the evil. Seasoned prophets have broad intelligence on such matters and are able to identify the forces with or against them. They skillfully cooperate with or counter their maneuvers.

For instance, church prophets spot and identify the problems with nouveau, scripturally unfounded doctrine or worship forms that undoubtedly steer congregations away from God's holiness. They bring the balance between praise and worship and solid Bible teaching. The devil can take a church off its Christ emphasis by pumping up praise and singing to the point that week after week all the church does is sing and dance. In the beginning the change may be good, but after awhile it grows old, showing itself as a subtle trick to keep the Bible and Bible teaching out of the church. I have been to services where the church was proud of its praise being so powerful that they never had time for the word of God. I reacted with concern, recognizing the remark as the stage one tactic to making the church powerless. Prophets know that this is not God, as it is only by His word that people grow and are grounded in His truth. Over time, sensuality replaced spirituality and the congregation never noticed when it took place. All they know is they that have become tired of singing and want to be fed the word of God. It is an old tactic, but a highly effective one.

Prophetic wisdom and knowledge enables prophets to inform, if not persuade, their churches of the inevitable outcomes and consequences of neo theology and risky ventures. They easily detect wolves in sheep's clothing. Their service object is always (or should be) God's truth, holiness, and righteousness in the Holy Spirit. True prophets trumpet these words as divine commands incessantly. The wholesomeness of the Lord's purchased possession emerges as uppermost in resident church's minds. For this to happen, the church prophet must be well versed in God's Holy Scriptures, and far too many are not.

Bible knowledge skills add reach and depth to the revelatory word of

God when merged with their assignments. It also enhances their prophetic accuracy. Otherwise *scripture light* prophets just declare releases of the people's heart desires more than they unfurl divine revelation. Thus their revelatory emphasis can be restricted to the congregation's most pressing temporal needs and fluctuating emotional states. The membership's spiritual state of well-being is generally ignored under such circumstances.

The fruit of such church prophetics is perceivable because it, like the Laodiceans, appears as a materially rich carbon copy of the world you thought you left behind. They are worldly in their views with a totally *here and now* mentality. Prophets who share like perspectives will no doubt enjoy a prominent position in these churches. However, in the end, like the prophets of Jeremiah 23 and Micah 3:5–12, neither of the two will prosper each other.

The Church Prophet's Chief Resource—God's Eternal Word

Many people enjoy hearing prophetic words of material possessions and supernatural deliverance from routine trials. However, there is a depth of the prophetic God wishes His prophets to bring into their houses that far exceeds the "bless you because you are blessed" words most of us have sought. There is a hallowed priestly tinge to the prophetic word that springs from, or uses abundantly, the scriptures. The prophet who uses them unfolds the Lord's timeless connection between the hearer's call and redemption and the Creator's will for their lives on earth.

Moreover, scripture integration in prophetic messages further renews Christians to God. Life is difficult and the trials that bring out God's best in us are painful. Those who go through years of bitter trials can get weary as their fires wane. Their souls can get thirsty from the dry, parched existence they live as they barely hold on to God's word. Such people then need prophets to reignite and revive their passion for God's service and sacrifice. That reviving, according to Psalm 119, can only come from the Lord's word. Prophet's who rely on scriptures for their prophecies will find the Lord unfolding the pages of people's lives right before their eyes using ancient texts about which they had previously wondered if they were for today.

Personal Prophecy and People's Life Book

Since the Bible tells us that God wrote a book for all of us, it comes as no surprise that behind every prophetic encounter there is a Creator revelation. Nor should it be difficult for prophets of this era to accept that they do not have to manufacture the word of the Lord for His people. Psalm 139:16 emphatically states that God wrote down the days of peoples' lives before they began. The psalmist understood, for example, how his life would turn out because what the Lord had written before his birth concerning him was revealed. It is accepted that David was also a prophet and so his ability to discern the Lord's eternal writings and interpret them for his existence on earth is credible. God even wrote about those who would reject Christ before time began and penned this truth for our time. Psalm 37:13,18 says this, and throughout the Bible it is recorded how the Lord wrote a book for this or that.

God wrote the book of life, the book of the generations of Adam, the book of the generation of Christ. There is the book of the wars of the Lord, the book of the law of God, and the books of blessings and curses. God has books on kings, kingdoms, nations, and judgments. The most common ones are the books of His prophets. He had His prophets write numerous books to chronicle His dealings with humanity and their diverse reactions to it throughout the years. Their writings included God's reactions, as well as the detailed judgments that correspond to their crimes against Him. When the priests of ancient Israel failed Him, the Lord wrote a book of remembrance to record the special deeds of those who courageously feared Him under the Mosaic dispensation. See this in Malachi 3.

The Bible mentions books in one way or another nearly two hundred times. In the vast majority of those references, the books contained prophecies. Apparently, that many references to books and records say the Lord's respect for earthly as well as heavenly records are important to Him. In the New Testament, John's Apocalypse discusses books in relation to the activities of God at least twenty-five times. Overall, God's books contain the governmental guidelines His spiritual protocrats are using to administrate His will on earth. Genre like end-time prophecy and the second coming of Christ, the records of the living and the dead, the deeds of each group, and how the Creator disposes of the earth and its godless inhabitants in the end comprise its subject matter.

Scripture's discussion of books was not just to show how important records are to the Lord, but also to reveal the prophet's source of information. The Lord's library provides the intelligence they need to prophesy His words to others at the appointed times. That is how and why personal prophecies are biblical.

Since the Lord wrote a book on every soul He ever created, there are eternal and temporal plans for each one of us. Those born on earth begin their journey according to scripture in the book of Adam. See Genesis 5:1. Upon salvation, a person's life plan comes from the book of the generation of Christ (see Matthew 1:1). The writer of Hebrews understood this because he made reference to it in Hebrews 10:7. Psalms 22 and 110 in like manner are excerpts from the eternal books written about the Christ and so His generation. Actually, that is what Isaiah means when he asks the question about who will declare Christ's generation (see Isaiah 53:8).

Long before His incarnation, Abraham saw the Christ and his vision was written before His time. Jesus made reference to Abraham's pre-carnate revelations of Himself as the Son of God when disputing with the religious leaders of His day in John 8:56. Not only was Abraham, a recognized prophet of the Most High God (according to Genesis 20:7), privy to the Son of God's day, but Genesis 15–18 record his viewing the entire plan of salvation for his seed when they had yet to be born. His revelation is referred to in Galatians 3:8, a New Testament book. Even what Daniel received from the mouth of the angel Gabriel was from the eternal scripture of God. Gabriel called it "the scripture of truth" (Daniel 10:21). That is why the apocalypse and all the other prophetic revelations of the Lord could be written in their times. They already existed and were waiting for their designated vessels to be born, live life, and be cultivated enough to pen the next body of revelation the Lord had for the world.

Scripture tells us each generation has a revelation to divulge because the Lord called His generations from the beginning and formed them for his various works and assignments in their times. Read Isaiah 41:4.

The Generations of Adam

Adam's generations are many, as the Bible uses the plural form of the word in relation to his offspring. It is plural because they keep dying out. Christ's offspring, in comparison, is one continuous world-without-end generation. It is singular because there is only one way in Him, and His seed lives forever. Eternal life requires an eternal plan to cover every inch of the person's everlasting existence. Therefore, the Lord precedes our destinies with His plan for how we will live.

Prophecies concerning Adam's generations are earthly and therefore soulish when they are not derived from God's Spirit revelation of His eternal plan for them. At times, the Lord will release a futuristic word to a prophet on an unsaved life so that the forces assigned to seeing to its redemption are informed of the path God is taking with them. Thus, a baby may be told that they will be this or that, or an unsaved person may hear from the prophet the reason why they were born, why the Lord wants to redeem them, and His plans for them after they receive Jesus Christ. However, in the absence of God's interjection, Adam's seeds rarely hear from the true and living God. What they get from the supernatural are chiefly soul-pleasing things. That is why the psychics can *seem* to have as much knowledge about people as God's prophets, although they really do not. The difference is the source of information retrieved from the supernatural that they deliver.

Being lost themselves, psychics are limited to getting their readings from the soul realm and not the Spirit. They will never be able to divine what the Lord has hidden in Christ's book on a life because that information must be spiritually discerned. Hence, the key difference between prophecy and divination is that the prophet speaks by the Lord's Spirit information that only the Creator can release to His redeemed. Psychic divinations comes from any spirit (divine being) that happens to be in the vicinity of the persons uttering and receiving the reading.

From all this, it is safe to conclude that what the prophets of God spoke they received from the Lord's eternal record of world events and His scripture on the generations of peoples' lives. What the occultists divine is another thing. It is what is contained in Adam's book and so restricted to life on earth period, for tomorrow, they die, the end. Now we shift our discussion to prophecy itself and what it is.

What Prophecy Is

As alluded to several times before, prophecy is God's divine communications media, His means of making His inaudible self audible and his invisible self visible. Prophecy is not a vain imagination of the vocalizer, but a medium by which the earth can hear from and be guided by its Creator. As we have seen, prophecy is actually a prophet's ability to read the life book of the one standing before them. That is what the preceding section took great pains to stress.

Prophecy is really receiving information from God on a person's life or situations from eternity and manifesting His word on it in our natural world. What's more, prophecy is encoded in everyday life and in all creation's existence. When the prophet speaks the word of the Lord, it comes to pass because it has been incubating in the spirit realm for years waiting for the predetermined time and lineage to appear in natural form. Amos 3:7 is a popular verse of prophecy, but it is verse 8 that enlarges our understanding of its power. Both verses establish that the Lord speaks what He is about to do prophetically somewhere to some prophet to start the processes that materialize His word on earth. When He speaks, He impels His prophets to prophesy because that is the reason He permitted them to hear His thoughts in the first place. The word for the secrets the Lord reveals to His prophets in Amos 3:7 is *sod*.

Summarily, *sod* applies to the supernatural act of God whereby He brings the spirits of every prophet into a private, usually midnight or twilight, meeting with Himself. *Sod* meetings are closed chamber sessions where His prophets convene with His supernatural military, governmental, judicial, and punitive agents for a special move or work to take place on earth. As used in Amos 3:7, the word refers to private council deliberations between God and His prophets' spirits where He communicates His will and unveils His plans to them to declare at the proper time. The following chapter discusses prophecy to give you insight on how it works and where it originates.

Chapter 9

PROPHECY CLASS 101

This chapter contains a brief prophecy class to help you appreciate what prophecy is and where it originates. Many people have had so much fun enjoying prophecy that they have given little thought to where it comes from and what makes it authoritative and reliable. Oftentimes, the hearing of prophecy alone is sufficient enough for people to delight in it. Few people realize that more than pleasant or inspiring words being said is happening. Many are willing to believe or do not know that the pronouncement of prophecy sets in motion a host of powers and events that can initially shake up a person's life before the word comes to pass. The shake-up happens in order to materialize what the word of the Lord promised in its time. Hindering forces, misguided ideas and beliefs, and the presence of detrimental relationships in one's sphere of life can delay the performance of God's words.

God's spiritual diligence goes into action once the word of the Lord has gone forth to clear the way for its manifestation. Sometimes this can be very upsetting, and occasionally excruciating. In addition, the opposing forces seeking to retain what they have held from you for so long are aroused. In a knee-jerk reaction they form invisible barricades that block the flow of spiritual resources your life needs to empower your faith enough to evidence the prophecy. These are not passive forces mind you. They may have been silent when there was no contest for your faith, but once prophecy comes they go into fierce action to see the word does not come to pass in your life, or that you are in the wrong place to receive it. Their goal is for you to leave the place for God's promises to come to pass for you, or have you miss it because you were never there at its fulfillment. If this happens, another person enjoys your blessing, your children, ministry offspring, etc. It is somewhat like what took place with the children of Israel.

The first generation that came out of Egypt did not receive the promise because they feared its conditions—attacking the giants in the land. On top of that, they made the mistake of following the wrong (usually counterfeit) prophetic voice. Even though Moses had led them for years and was the established voice of the Lord for them, they turned and listened to others who presumed to know better than Moses the Lord's plan for them. Today we see this happening often, as people hear the word of God and fearing its costs and consequences turn to another voice to get a prophecy they can live with, one that has less strings attached to it. Similar fears caused the apostle Paul to tell Timothy to wage spiritual warfare with (and over) his prophetic word to provoke its performance in his life. See 1 Timothy 1:18.

Prophecy Class
Prophecy Is What Exactly?

How many times have you heard that question? The majority of the time, the answer is simply the word of the Lord. While that is true, it seems to come short of the answer most people look to receive. They want an explanation that fosters their understanding of the medium of prophecy so they properly handle the prophetic words they get. For those people, a somewhat more intricate response is needed. When New Creation faith and godly reason mix, the result is spiritual intelligence in the supernatural ways and wisdom of God. Hence, prophecy is the Lord's word performed, achieved, and mobilized in the spirit, soul, and body of its believers. As the invisible eternal word of God spoken in the natural world, it operates what He deposited in creation to perform or fulfill something He wants to be.

Prophecy involves the past, present, and the future respectively and interchangeably. It takes spiritual faculties to hear, see, dream, and otherwise receive from Creator God's spiritual creation. And a special attunement of the normal human faculties is needed for prophetic types to receive their messages. To assure what one receives from the spirit realm is prophetic and not psychic, review the section on the seventh sense.

Prophecy is normally spontaneous and can be predictive, revelatory, didactic, literary, or oracular. That means, the prophetic can manifest itself through: *foretelling, forthtelling, teaching, writings, or verbal utterances under the inspiration of the Spirit of God.*

As a medium, prophecy's purpose is to reveal the invisible mind and dispense the material provisions of God to His visible world. As a tool, it is the vehicle by which the Lord enables humans to access His invisible form. Once someone has gained access to heaven's hidden treasuries, prayer and belief in prophetic utterances shape and conform their request to divine purpose. Sustained, these ultimately attract and adorn the petition's natural physique and appearance in our world. Here is what Paul meant by his counsel to Timothy in 1:18 and 1:14. It is what happened when Christ cursed the fig tree, when Elisha summoned a child for the Shunnamite woman, and when Jesus multiplied the fishes and the loaves. Based on His covenant and comprehension of His Father's ways, they were already in existence, awaiting His command.

The Power of a Prophetic Mindset

The key to accomplishing such great feats is a prophetic mindset. That is an ongoing realization that what you want and need from God already exists in your kingdom account and all you need to do is withdraw it from the supernatural and embody it in the natural realm. Many things go into making this happen on purpose and on command. Mark 11:24 hints at it. It says if you believe what you ask for, you will have it. The Greek word for this is *esomai*, and it literally means "will be." The term implies that your belief will cause it to exist. While there is much more to say on this subject, for now suffice it to say that essentially this is what Christ is talking about when He said whatever you ask in my name I will do. The word for "will do" is *poieo*, and it actually has Jesus saying He will prepare, construct, acquire, fashion, and author it.

As the Logos, the word, intelligence, and power that created all things, He gave us a clue to how to bring what He and His Father prepared for us from the foundation of the world into view and use. That clue is proclamation of His word and declaration of one's desires. Read Job 28:27, which is based on Job 22:28.

A special collaborative arrangement between the Lord and His prophets accomplished through their uniquely empowered spirits enables their commands to cause their words to appear in natural form. You only need to read 2 Chronicles 20:20 and Isaiah 44:26 to be persuaded by this truth. God's declaration that He reveal His works and plans to and through His prophets is a tremendous statement. They are more than His voice boxes; they are His implements and instruments as well. Review Hosea 6:5 and Zechariah 1:6. Below are some of the functions and objectives for prophecy and God's uses of it:

- Destiny
- Ministry
- Correction
- Blessing
- Admonishment
- Change
- Creation

- Healing
- Power
- Possession and dispossession
- Instruction
- Counsel
- Impartation
- Empowerment

Where Prophecy Originated

As we explained previously, prophecy comes from the Creator. What makes it prophecy according to definition is its sphere of formation. That is eternity. When God says anything, it is prophetic because He spoke it outside of our time to be manifested in our eras. Here is why prophecy relies much on dreams and visions. These mechanisms of divine communication are not time bound, even if the dreamer receives them in a given day or night. Because they are images depicting what God is doing or wants to do, provided they are prophetic of course, the messages emanate from eternity and are outside of time even if they are alive in the dreamer's mind. It is like the sperm and egg that make a baby. They always existed as potential people in the man and woman's bodies, but are not time relevant until they are first conceived. After gestation and birth into the world, the child is subject to its tempo. As long as a baby is in the womb, it is exempt from time and its ordinances as we know them. It lives, is alive, and is a person, but it is not on life's clock—the timepiece of earthly life. Once it is born, it receives a birth date and becomes subject to the laws and processes of the earth. So it is with prophecy.

By definition prophecy is *pro*—"beforehand" or "time"—and *phemi* (or *phani*)—"saying"—that which is said before it happens. Inasmuch as the Lord created and formed all we see, feel, hear, and touch outside time, every element of human existence may be seen as prophetic or a manifestation of prophecy. The Genesis account of creation supports this.

Before the world was, God said, "Let there be." The Bible goes on to tell us that what He declared to be came forth, because the record says, "and it was so." This truth is upheld in 2 Peter 3:5, a reiteration of Psalm 33:6 and Hebrew 11:3.

Once the Lord God spoke what He wanted to appear, He observed its formation and outworking from eternity as it moved from there to here. In eternity, things manifest at the speed of God and not man. With His word not being confined to our time clocks and calendars, it was not a problem for Him to create His world in a week. Afterward, He assigned everything its time, season, purpose, vessel, genealogy, and history. Still working from heaven and earth at once, He then recorded in eternity the events that unfolded in His chronicles. From then it was all set in motion (albeit a drastically slowed down motion) to be lived out in the flesh.

The Lord has given us this same formula to repeat what He did in our own world and lives. Hence, prophecy mirrors God's beforehand record of what took place at the speed of eternity, now unfolding in us in time, age to age, before it appeared on earth. Even the variables of human free will are known by God because for the most part what we do at a snail's pace compared to eternity was done under His observation before He placed us in our clay vessels on the planet. Prophets then get their information from the spirit realm, the Holy Spirit who communicates select portions and pieces of the Creator's divine record to them at prescribed periods in history.

Prophetic revelations come from the pages of human lives in Adam and those in Christ. They divulge the Lord's purposes for our existence as only He can know it. At any given stage in human, earthly, and individuals' histories, the Lord can open a page of a person's book and reveal it to His prophet. This is in addition to, but aside from, the normal operation of prophetic faculties that render prophet's the ability to pierce the veil of the flesh and detect what is happening in the future. Prophets do this routinely as part of their occupational duties to the Lord.

Expanded Prophetic Abilities

Extended prophetic information comes from the overt and direct actions of the citizens of the supernatural world. The Bible identifies these beings as the angels of the Lord. In ancient times for example, it was accepted that a dream angel caused all prophetic dreams. The expansion of a prophet's mantle determines the spherical range of his or her prophetic reach and aptitude. The mantle as it appears to the invisible world says whether the prophet's supernatural faculties can operate on a local, national, international, or even stratospheric level.

Many new prophets are limited in their prophecy scope and range. They can only receive tiny fragments of what a seasoned prophet can retrieve from the spirit realms of God. Purposely, God restricts the breath and level of prophetic information the prophet either receives or comprehends. He does this by contracting their prophetic orb to minimize their access to His spirituality and thereby control the breadth of their prophecies. The reason the Lord does this most is time developmental. It helps him refine their skill, fine tune their prophetic receptors, and qualify their prophetic motivations. At other times it is punitive. When prophets have a constant track record of ignoring Him or perverting His words, He shuts their lights off. Micah 3:6–7 describes it as follows:

> **Therefore night shall be unto you, that ye shall not have a vision; and it shall be dark unto you, that ye shall not divine; and the sun shall go down over the prophets, and the day shall be dark over them. Then shall the seers be ashamed, and the diviners confounded: yea, they shall all cover their lips; for there is no answer of God.**

What can make the Lord curtail or cut off entirely a prophet's ability so that their prophetics have to resort to demons to operate Micah also explains:

Her leaders judge for a bribe, her priests teach for a price, and her prophets tell fortunes for money. Yet they lean upon the Lord and say, "Is not the Lord among us? No disaster will come upon us."

—Micah 3:11 (NIV)

Technical Prophetic Information

In an effort to provide a solid biblical basis for prophecy, here is a lecture that anatomizes it for the prophet who wants to thoroughly grasp the mind of God on prophetics.

Anatomy of Prophecy

One word for prophecy helps us understand its meaning, the purpose it serves, and its aim. Found in 1 Chronicles 9:25, it is the word *nebuwah* and means "a prediction given orally or in writing." It defines a specific prophetic word whether true or false. Another prophecy term employed in the Old Testament is *naba*. You may also see it spelled *nava*. This word is a verb for "to prophesy." As a root term it identifies prophesying in song. *Naba* can apply to psalmism or a predictive discourse lyrical or not through a genuine or false prophet. Whichever is the case, the gist is that the message delivered is unquestionably under the direct influence of a divine spirit. See 1 Chronicles 15:8 and Nehemiah 6:12.

For the *nabi* prophet, which we discussed at length elsewhere, Daniel 9:24 is one good scriptural reference. It defines *nabi* as "a prophet, a person who is an inspired messenger." The word includes "the specifically declared prophecy that comes from the *official* prophet as the spokesperson of a deity true or false." When the *nabi* pertains to prophesying, it stresses the prophetic message that specifically comes from the one in the prophet's office that when uttered establishes the messenger as an authentic prophet.

Another helpful word for prophecy that is especially significant answers the experience of the weight of the prophetic word from the Lord. It is identified in scripture as a prophetic burden. The word is *massa,* and Proverbs 30:12 and 31:1 both distinguish it as "prophecy that is carried as a burden." *Massa* transmits the essence of what we would call a prophetic burden as a weighty word from the Lord. Such prophecy flows from an accompanying spiritual charge from the Lord that is felt with the natural senses. It is recognized by utterances in definitive, concrete, or symbolic terms. Generally, *massa* prophecy is likely to use figurative (parabolic) language that expresses God's intellectual desires or reflects the prophet's intelligent cognition of a cause that is ultimately translating to an effect or consequence. In the message, the prophet is moved by spiritual and godly aspirations. Often a *massa* burden is characterized by a message of doom, although not exclusively.

New Testament Prophecy

In the New Testament only two words are used for prophecy. One of them is used three times. It is the word *prophetikos,* that defines "what proceeds from a prophet as prophetic." The ending, *ikos,* sets the word's meaning in the arena of technique. It covers more than the prophet's prophesying and encompasses the full range of supernatural and revelatory activities that identify the office. *Prophetikos* not only constitutes prophecy as known and recognized by the people of God, but encapsulates the behind the scenes outworking of the prophet's word that manifests prophecy in its literal form.

Prophetikos also refers to foretelling prophecy and the corresponding operations that cement its prediction or unveil its revelation. Demonstrative prophetic techniques are likely to follow the word such as dance, imagery, drama, poetry, or rhyme to depict its symbolism. See Romans 16:26 where the term is used twice in one verse. The last usage comes from 2 Peter 1:19.

Every other term the New Testament uses for prophecy falls under the meaning of the word *propheteia*. Basically this word defines a prophecy whether it comes from mere recitation of scripture or from an outright spontaneous utterance from the present mind of God. The *propheteia* word declares God's thoughts, feelings, reactions, and emotional responses on earthly affairs and human matters. Prophecy of this kind typically links to some future event where the matters or affairs divulged are complemented with some divine action on God's part. In short, signs appear shortly before or after the word leaves the prophet's mouth. Since they come from God, He is the one who releases the prophetic sign that seals the certain performance of the word spoken by His prophets. The sign may be displayed by the prophet, but more often it is a sign the Lord Himself gives to quicken to the mind of the hearer that the prophecy is authentic and will surely come to pass.

One example is the occurrence of an event that seems unrelated to anything in the person's life or experience triggered by and related to the prophecy. Prophetic signature is totally consistent with the Old Testament prophet's words that brought us to the New. Isaiah 7:14 orientates us to the reality that prophetic signs confirmed the Lord's word as in the coming crucifixion and resurrection of our Lord Jesus Christ.

Propheteia includes the Creator's appropriation of the prophet's spirit, the source of the messenger's predictive ability, and revelatory sight. It contemporaneously pertains to didactic prophetics where teaching permeates the prophet's discourse to combine the wisdom of the now in Christ with the insightful predictions of ancient prophets to reveal Him. Predictive and didactic prophecy joins instruction to unfold the existence, purposes, and work of His church on earth. Didactic prophetic predictions foretell how and where the church, its ministers, and its operations empowered by the Holy Spirit are to manifest their reach and demonstrate the powers of the Living God as Christ's representative. Luke 24:44-49 is an example, as is Matthew 10, the training commissioning of the apostles, and Luke 10 where the seventy were likewise dispatched.

Prophetic Teaching and Preaching

Aside from bringing the word of the Lord, one of the most intriguing things about prophetic ministry is its distinct style of sermonic delivery. According to Romans 12 where the gift of prophecy is mentioned, revelatory and predictive influences are typical of the mantle. The prophet's style of sermonizing incorporates several spiritual and supernatural features that help stimulate hearers' understanding. With their sometimes humorous and pragmatic way of speaking, prophets frequently integrate symbolism, parables, and similitudes in their messages to instruct and invigorate their audiences. The prophet's spirit combined with its inherent actuating force, amplifies this fundamental gift. The capability enables the prophet to also perceptively rotate between teaching and prophesying as the tenor and mix of the audience requires. That is to say that prophets can slip into predicting something to come to pass or casually reveal something otherwise concealed in God while preaching. Our Savior often used this technique to communicate the fullness of the gospel message His Father sent Him to preach. Luke 4:23 and 13:4 are good examples of such sermonizing.

Prophets also easily take God's ancient word and apply it to modern situations. Here is another capacity of their unique teaching and preaching ability. What may seem old and outdated to the typical Bible reader is not so with the prophet. This unusual minister sees past, present, and future in one sweep, looking at life through the word of the Lord. They compare it to what they observe in the world around them. To the prophet, the chariot is not merely outmoded transportation; it is a vehicle regardless of its shape and engine. Prophets can see how the ancient chariot that was used in transport or battle way back in time symbolizes today's modern tank. Likewise the bow and arrow. Rigid thinkers can easily overlook the fact that they are weapons of war nonetheless. So when they read the scriptures, they allow themselves to be locked into the ear in which the word is reporting, not the prophet. He or she sees the events that led up

to war as an example for us today. They identify the attitudes and conduct of the war and the way the weapons were fired whether powered by
humans or nuclear energy. For instance, it has been said that David's
stone that slew Goliath was a guided missile. David threw it, but God's
hand guided it to its target.

Prophets can also take the practical and spiritual doctrines of the
Lord's word and update them using contemporary imagery and metaphors. Anointed prophetic wisdom makes hearers see how what prophets
say and teach really does fit modern situations. To the prophet, sophistication is but a remake of the antiquated. They echo Solomon's sentiment, "there is nothing new under the sun, and that which is has already
been" (Ecclesiastes 1:10; 3:15).

Final Notes on the Basics of Prophecy

1. **Amos 3:7**—*Emphasis:* The meaning of the word *sod.*
   - The word for the secrets God reveals to His servants the
     prophets.
   - *Sod* distinguishes prophetic hearing from the range of spiri-
     tual hearing the Holy Spirit allows.
   - *Sod* designates the official character of the prophetic
     message's delivery system as what God uses exclusively with
     prophets.
   - *Sod* centers on the deliberations that take place among high
     officials in closed chamber sessions.
   - *Sod* relates the distinctives of the prophet's means of revela-
     tion and grounds for perceptions to the sphere of prophetics
     they operate within.
2. **2 Chronicles 20:20**—*Emphasis:* The powerful prosperity
   anointing inherent to the prophet's mantle.
   - This scripture establishes how and why the prophet's power
     extends to the sphere of prosperity.

- Prophecy is prosperity's means in the world of prophetics.
- The benefit and basis of the prosperity link to money and triumph.
- It says how and why prophets are instrumental in triumph.
- It answers how the previous statement relates to Amos 3:7.
- The word "prosperity" actually means, promises, and provides in relation to how the word of the Lord is treated today more than money.

3. **Psalm 139:15–16**—*Emphasis:* The eternal writings of Creator God.

- That God wrote it all down in advance.
- Foreknowledge means that the Lord wrote it all down in eternity for prophecy to manifest in time.
- God's writings translate to prophecy.
- What the Lord wrote in advance affects the events of the lives of those He recorded in His prophetic ordinations.
- Hebrews 10:7 exemplifies that a volume of the book in which each of our lives are recorded exists. It is how and why its variables are accounted for and yet remain immutable for prophets to declare.

4. **Numbers 12:6**—*Emphasis:* The visions and dreams used to induct prophets into office.

- Visions and dreams are the primary medium of prophetic induction.
- Dreams and visions are decidedly the best way to awaken the prophet's spirit.
- What makes prophets inherently susceptible to God's spiritual activation is their prophet's spirit.
- The passage contributes to, complements, and supports the prophetic's reception and transmission.

5. **Acts 15:18**—*Emphasis:* Eternity and time are known to God.

· This links to Hebrews 10:7 and Psalm 139:15–16.

Prophetic Prayer

Needless to say, more than any other minister in the New Testament church, the prophet's chief responsibility must be prayer. Prayer for the prophet is above prophesying, for without prayer the prophecies the prophet gives may not be totally accurate, relevant, or timely. Prayer synchronizes the prophet's clock and perspectives with God's. It unites their supernatural self with the supernatural forces assigned to their work on earth. Prayer opens the heavens, removes the darkness, and shed's God's light on matters prophets handle. A shabby prayer life eventually renders prophets feeble in their ministries and hinders the execution of their prophetic duties.

The reason prayer is so vital has to do with the weighty intercessory obligation of the messenger. The prophet's primary charge, if you recall, is to stand in the gap and make up the hedge for God's people on earth. This responsibility is where Israel's prophets fail in Ezekiel 13:5. But what is it for the prophet to pray?

According to the Bible, there is no more effective prayer group than that of prophets and apostles, collectively and respectively. I used to wonder about this until I had opportunity to observe and experience the difference. When prophets pray with others, they may have a productive prayer time. However, when they pray with their peers of like spirit, the results are explosive. Their respective mantles coagulate and each one's anointing power is magnified a thousand-fold. When this group gets together, the time it takes to transcend the world and flesh is milliseconds in comparison to other prayer groups.

Prophets do not need the long spiritual prologues, extensive meditation, or empty praise fillers normally required by others before they transition from the human to the heavenly. In an instant, prophet's seasoned spirits leap onto God's plane ready to do business as He needs. Prophets further understand what to expect from their prayer vigils and approach them with a confident determination to plow through everything in their way. With other prayer groups it is different. Their spiritual immaturity or weakness can lag behind in the spirit as they are unaccustomed or unable to shake off the flesh that holds down their spiritual power. Many believers frequently lack the fortitude to push in the spirit and are easily driven back to carnality at the hint of demonic resistance. Prophetic prayer groups, on the other hand, are able to confront and conquer the spiritual bullies the devil assigns to their gatherings. They enter the prayer with a sense of assignment, duty, and invincibility. Prophets are not quickly or easily cowered in prayer and over time resolve to outgrow weaknesses that make them vulnerable to such tactics in the future.

Once on God's plane, prophets are attuned to His most intimate thoughts, being experienced in conceiving what the Lord wants to deposit in them. The prayer prophet's company immediately transforms their environment to a battlefield, revelation hub, military camp, worship, and praise center. Throughout the prayer, the group travels all these stages to make happen on earth what the Lord has shown them in heaven. Before tackling other issues, the prophet comes to God to be healed, cleansed, empowered, and impregnated. They are conditioned to conceive His thoughts, commune with His word, and be further transformed into His image and likeness. Prophets not only seek this from their prayer times, they expect and insist that the Lord grants them this fruit. When the prayer is ended, the room is changed to a sanctuary. The glory is present and the word of the Lord is flowing abundantly.

It is sad that the least communal prayer group in the body of Christ tends to be the leaders, prophets, and apostles most importantly. I have witnessed how pastors and church leaders rise to fame and begin to see prayer as beneath them. They know how to reach God but have assigned special groups to do it for them. Unless there is a crises, far too many of the churches of the Lord Jesus replace valuable prayer time with works while still relying on the Lord's Spirit to support them in their ventures.

Biblical prophetic prayer models are Samuel, Moses, David, Daniel, Job, Abraham, and others, to name a few. What these all share are their conviction for intercession. Many times active prophetic prayer can halt or derail an attack of the enemy meant to overthrow the plans and purposes of God. When prophets enter active prayer, visions flood their mind. The Lord's thoughts stream at them at accelerated rates as their spirits overwhelm their natural self. At this time the Lord's broadest and most finite matters are divulged and the *sod* meeting begins. The messengers hear God's plan, understand the strategy, and are enlightened on the targets of their next prophetic assignment. From all this, you can see how prophets prayer lives are important to accuracy and effectiveness.

Another unique feature of prophetic prayer groups is recognizing that fault and failure for life's crises lie with humans and not with the Lord. Prophets differ from other groups because they never assign blame to the Lord or wrangle His word to excuse human behavior. Rather, prophets are aware that sin problems reside with humans. Therefore they include in their intercessory sessions, vicarious repentance for the sins of the people of the lands they pray for and then proceed to use their authority to release their blessings. Daniel's intercession in chapters 9 and 10 shows this. An overall praying prophet is a most valuable tool in public ministry. Without prophetic prayer, the institution of prophecy is only marginally effective. See pastor's prayer life in Acts 2.

The Prophecy Anointing

It might be helpful to church prophets and their pastors to know about the prophecy anointing as it streams from the baptism of the Holy Spirit. The name of the anointing that empowers Christ's ministers for their service to the Lord is *chrio*. As an aspect of the Lord's many anointings, this one is distinct in that it may also be called the ministry power anointing. *Chrio* describes the outpouring of the Holy Spirit that specifically rests on His officers and ministers in active service. *Chrio* furnishes what is needed to perform the duties and exploits of one's call.

According to *Strong's Concordance,* the word *chrio* is used four times in the New Testament. Only one of those times is it applied outside of Christ, which is not to say that it does not apply to human ministers because that is inaccurate. What it is to say though, is that the *chrio* anointing specifically empowers divine service. The single time the word *chrio* is rendered anointing for human ministers is in 2 Corinthians 1:21 in relation to the apostles. However, what makes it relevant to us today is that Jesus was sent to earth as the first Minister of the New Covenant. He came as the Prophet who was to come and the Great Apostle. All this states that the *chrio* anointing to minister is more than the *chrisma* all believers get. It goes along with Acts 1:8 where the Lord instructs His followers to remain in Jerusalem until they are endued with power from on high in Luke 24:49. Otherwise, it is only used in the New Testament one other time.

Without *chrio*, ministers rely entirely on their human talents and have a lesser degree of potency and consequently ministry success. *Chrio* is a power anointing, period. It comes upon the Lord's servants for one reason, and one reason only: to empower them as effective witnesses of God's word, truth, and power. Because of this goal, *chrio* also supplies what it takes to yield to the moves and waves of the Holy Spirit. Without it, Christ's ministers cannot quite submit to God's will, be used by His power, or execute what cannot ordinarily be done by mortal humans. The anointing when manifested in this context uses the vessel rather than the normal course of affairs where we use the anointing in ministry. To clarify the distinctions between the *chrio* anointing and the others, in matters and tasks of routing nature the vessel, the minister, uses the anointing, or employs it, which is a better way of saying it. *Chrio* uses the vessel.

The connection between the Lord and His ministers under these circumstances is rigid and distinct. Enormous latitude and trust is accorded those whom Jesus baptizes with His *chrio* anointing. Their obedience must firmly be established and their motives and agenda beyond suspicion. These being confirmed, the Lord imparts *chrio*'s powerful authority and potency because without it those called to His service would fail in the face of the severe trials and contests associated with ministry.

The Prophetic and *Chrio*

With the prophetic, the *chrio* anointing is centered primarily in the dispensation of prophecy, although not exclusively. Several noticeable sensations can accompany the onset of the prophecy anointing. Jeremiah spoke of quaking, burning, weakness, or loss of strength. Daniel spoke of, in relation to the prophecy anointing, a heaviness that weighed him down and something akin to passing out—what we call today being slain in the spirit. The other prophets voice a distinct weight placed upon them that they identified as the hand of the Lord upon them to prophesy. Usually they felt this in the shoulder, neck, and back area, as the term yoke is synonymous with mantle. Others identified the *massa* prophetic burden for the oracle. While such sensations are not essential to prophecy, the Bible often mentions the weight of prophetic oracle being felt by the prophet. It seemed to be its heaviest when the message was being deposited in the prophet for later utterance.

The Source of Prophetic Power

People invariably ask what makes the prophet's words come to pass. Although much discussion has alluded to the answer, below are the concrete things that assure a prophet's word will come to pass.

The source of prophetic power is summed up at as follows:

- **The prophetic word itself.** The Lord's empowerment of the prophet's spirit gives weight to his or her prophecy. The weight though imperceptible gives off an aura detected by the invisible forces of creation to cause them to take what the messenger says seriously and do it.

- The angelic guard. The team of angelic forces God deployed to the prophet's sphere at the time of the messenger's installation. They guard the work and enforce the prophet's word, powerfully imposing the Lord's will on the devil.

- Divine license to legitimately act. The spiritual certification and validation the Lord confers upon the prophet that authorizes him or her to act in supernatural matters within an assigned sphere. The license may not be discernible to humans, but it is recognized and respected by the forces of darkness. Divine license is generally uttered aloud from the mouth of the prophet while it is at the same time declared by God to His hosts. Jesus' instructions to the apostles in Matthew 10, along with His response to the return of the seventy's joy over their authority are two examples.

- Divine appointment to prophetic service. God may induct a prophet into His service privately, but He will cause that appointment to be recognized and honored by His leaders. More than once He will have it voiced in His seen and unseen worlds.

- An approved prophetic station. This is what Habakkuk referred to when he waited for God to answer him after his frustrated outburst over Israel's sin. He knew that he might be reproved because of it and a reproof from the Lord could be painful. Therefore, the prophet sought refuge in his prophetic ward, watch station. See Habakkuk 2:1.

- Approved prophetic assignment. The Lord's dispatch of the messenger with a message is what this means. The fact that the charge is given by God means that He will uphold it. What Moses received from his burning bush encounter with the Lord was a prophetic assignment.

Professional Prophetics

Professional prophets were a respectable guild of ministers once. They were particularly so in Mari. Look at some of the standards professional prophets of the day were held to in the ancient world. Professional prophetics were:

- Never undertaken by the novice or the unproved.
- Balanced by others in community groups of prophets.
- They generally had secluded quarters where group (and individual) encounters with the deity occurred.
- In addition, men and women were tried and proven for their positions.
- Women were seen as more visionary, men more vocal.
- Various forms of prophetic reception were employed.
- Prophetic reception required diverse actions for preparation.
- Various forms and styles of readiness were used.
- Numerous aspects of prophetic functions were dedicated to special prophetic vessels exhibiting exceptional prophetic aptitude.

Different vessels in the prophetic company were often employed by the deity in unique ways, and dispensed distinct technical manifestations that expressed its sentiment and will in matters. For instance, a comprehensive company of prophets may demonstrate their office in numerous ways, such as:

- Some only sang.
- Others only wailed.
- A few cried and wept in travail or as wailing vessels of the deity's sorrow or injury.
- Others ranted and raved as in spiritual warfare.
- Some decried and declared prophetic statements to illustrate

what the deity was doing with their petitions.

- Some entered into or acted out, or incited military strategy.
- Some simply peered into and uttered what was seen in the supernatural.
- Some summoned and actuated the supernatural with prayers, descriptive utterances, or authoritative commands.
- Some ecstatically worshipped until spiritual manifestations appeared.
- Some sacrificed animals to coax spiritual activity. Our Lamb has been sacrificed.
- Others imbibed various concoctions to stimulate and awaken their spiritual receptors to identify and define what the deity's spiritual hosts were doing. We are drunk with the Holy Spirit.
- Many simply offered prayers and fell asleep to receive instructions in the form of a vision or a dream.

Specific spiritual maneuvers were delegated each person to operate by a prophetic leader whose job it was to assure the prophetics of the group met with deity's approval.

The Psalmist and the Seer

Since not everyone exhibiting prophetic signs or uttering prophecy is an official prophet, the question becomes, what type of prophetic calling do they have on their life? The answer may be psalmist, if they sing their revelations and predictions frequently or rhyme them and exhibit no further prophetic conduct. Or, they may be a seer. This is likely if they regularly peer into the other world whether or not they can translate, enforce, or interpret what they see. Here are some features of each one:

The Psalmist:
- Singing prophet

- Prone to poetry
- Lyrical delivery
- Includes drama
- Often musical
- Impressive creativity
- Effective at rhyming
- Often literary
- Performs best with musical stimuli
- Potent praise accompany ministry

The Seer:

- Dreamer, visionary
- Supernatural sight
- Discerning detective spirit
- Strong interpretation likely
- May translate spiritual happenings
- Often can see and not be able to say or sometimes only can describe what is seen
- Visions shared often rely on recipient application of pictures to situations
- Symbolism and imagery interpretation may exist
- Definitive delivery style
- Confirming members of prophetic team

Quick Study Chart
Basics of the Prophet, Personality and Temperament

Prophets are characterized by consistent traits, attitudes, and behaviors that all prophets share to one degree or another. The chart below describes some commonalities that may help emerging prophets, pastors, and their flocks recognize a prophetic personality and better understand their unique temperament. Prophetic types across the board:

- Exhibit strong authoritative presence
- Predisposition to the prophetic's messenger office
- Easily motivated by the visions and dreams that induct into the ministry
- Compatible with the typically itinerant minister calling
- Relatively good minded
- Incisive and judicial in nature for prophet's leadership role
- Drive potent and provocative worshippers
- Suitable to serve as divine functionary via visions and dreams
- Naturally disposed inordinate divine communications
- Possess *nabiim* authority inclination
- Tend to be unavoidably detached loners
- Naturally discerning and probing
- Naturally oriented to the prophet's odd office requirements
- Daring, bold, outspoken
- Practical piercing and confrontational
- Scrupulously obedient to spiritual sways
- Possess an articulate ambassador spirit
- Tend to be a preaching teacher
- Compelling, corrective, chastening element due to impression of divine order
- Readily exert invocational power inherent in office

Portrait of Church Prophet Distinctives

What is very important in selecting a prophet of the church is an understanding of the qualities and traits that do not make for a compatible church prophet. As with any other organization's staff or department, God's prophets too come in an array of different designations. Some are designated to one level and others to a higher or lower one. Those levels may be national, community, global, or local. When it comes to the church prophet in the local church, it is best to install a prophet that is more home based minded than one with a national or international passion. Basic home body character in a person translates to a home body prophet. Your church prophet should not be elsewhere more than they are with you. They also should not resent having to be in church or actively involved in the spiritual life of your congregation, favoring their field ministry trips above all else.

You will know the home based prophet by his or her conversation. It is usually centered around the house of God, the condition of a specific congregation, and the importance of their presence in the church as a watchman for the Lord on the pastor's behalf. If a prophet's sights are more field minded than church minded, chances are that prophet will not do well confined to your church. Listen to their conversation and explore their ministry vision a bit before deciding to set them over your membership. While it might be glamorous to have a world prophet on staff, sound judgment indicates that global and national prophets are best used as advisors as they can make poor local church prophets. Their messages can be too above the people's heads far too often, and their visions for your church more for the corporate body of Christ. That means what God is issuing to the worldwide body could be dumped on your church, though it may not be applicable to it.

Besides this, the global or national prophet may be great for fortifying missions outreach from time to time, but when it comes to succoring the individual needs of the flock their issues may appear to the prophet petty in comparison. Such a prophet of the church could react callously, unintentionally or not, to the perceived as childish needs and plights of the local body. Lastly, the world class prophet may also come off, unwittingly, superior to the local pastor, deeming their vision and methods trite in contrast to the needs of the world front.

Following are some clues you may use to detect who is or is not a good church prophet candidate.

Quick Study Chart
Character Traits that Indicate Potential Church Prophet

- Stationary or demonstrate capacity for staying and functioning productively in one place
- Interested in a church, its members, and church vision
- Interacts positively and closely in a supportive role with headship
- Supports leadership actions and initiatives that are clearly the will of the Lord for the church
- Able to, and desirous of, guarding and supernaturally interceding on church's behalf
- Interested in superintending the spiritual activities of local church and diligently screening and upgrading its prophetic operations
- Demonstrating ability to function in full *nabiim* capacity
- Able to oversee prophetics, psalmism, intercessory prayer, and membership prophetic development
- Comfortable in collaborations with pastor in subordinate role on the welfare and prophetic benefits of mantle and ministry in church
- Open enough to introduce and promote new prophetic inflows and accurately screen those arising from local church midst
- Knowledgeable enough to evaluate active prophetics, confirm emerging prophets, and train prophets for in-house use and/or church dispatch to other areas
- Experienced enough to validate actuating prophetics and certify authenticity
- Shows leadership capacity harmonious with existing and emerging church leadership and government; able to diplomatically suggest prudent changes that better align the church with the kingdom of God

- Able to provide safe and reliable counsel to pastor confidentially
- Skillfully and productively interact with and *serve* the membership without undue familiarity that could color later prophetics
- Demonstrates an ability to be objective and easily detach self from the body to seek the Lord and still remain credible with leadership

To talk about the prophet in the church and neglect the officer's number one opposition, the occult, is derelict. The main reason why people find it difficult to reconcile God's need for the minister in contemporary times and especially in the New Testament church is because the reason God ordained prophets seems vague. People, as we have proven throughout this text, see the prophet as merely a vocalizer of future events. They see prophets as those who just speak God's words for no apparent reason. Herein lie the church's difficulty with the prophet, a difficulty the word and the spirits of darkness do not share. When thinking about the Lord's use of the prophet, one must consider the backdrop against which the Lord presents the officer to His people. That is the first clue we have as to why the Lord needs the prophet. Beginning with Abraham, also called in scripture a prophet, God initiates His method of getting His word and will into the earth and people's hearts. In an unprecedented battle between himself and the kings of the land, Abraham accomplished a monumental feat with the help of His God. He slaughtered the five kings, recaptured his family and treasures, and discovered the Almighty, the greatest of all gods, who becomes His covenant God. Following this comes Joseph, another scripture-declared prophet. His prophetic ability succeeded in placing him as the third leader in Egypt where he became the savior of his nation Israel through the use of his prophetic gifts.

When we see this method in operation again, it is with Moses whom God sent to deliver the people of Israel that the Lord brings us into the world of the prophetic. God talks to Moses from a burning bush and tells him what he is called to do. He is to display the Most High power to Pharaoh of Egypt and systematically dismantle powers of one of the oldest and most menacing kingdoms in history. Moses is to do so with only two resources, a wooden stick that he used to handle the flocks of Midian where he fled after killing an Egyptian officer forty years earlier, and a prophet. God told Moses that Aaron his brother would accompany him into Egypt and serve as Moses' prophet (spokesman for a deity). Moses would be to Aaron a god. With only two implements that transformed themselves into weapons of a cosmic war, the Lord toppled the entire Egyptian nation, bringing one disaster after another on them in a clash with every one of Israel's gods (see Numbers12:12). What is scarcely known about the Lord's church is that God Almighty through His prophet engaged the entire Egyptian pantheon in a contest and won a decisive victory. The history of the prophetic goes on as God continues His pattern with Joshua, Moses' successor.

Again, enlisting another supernatural agent to complete His project, God uses this militaristic prophet to conquer the territory Israel had been gathering. Joshua's prophetic mantle continues the legacy and is passed on after a few generations to Samuel, the prophet who instituted Israel's judgeship. Samuel blended into his mantle, judgeship, commander and chief, priest, and prophet. This four-fold gifting emerges as a developing model of diverse prophetic service. Samuel goes to war with the Philistines, calls the nation back to true worship, and restores devoted worship of Yahweh. Lastly, he organizes and formalizes prophetic education and ministry, propelling the nation forward in its destiny. God's prophetic mold continues as yet one other office merges with the office, that of king. After Saul's demise his replacement, David, assumes the role of prophet and priest (not unusual for monarchs of that day) along with roles previously anchored in the mantle by Samuel. David, a born warrior, exhibits a wholehearted working relationship between the Lord and

His prophet. He inquires of God and receives answers to what he asks by consulting the *ephod,* a kind of interrogatory vestment normally restricted to priests. Revelation becomes commonplace to this king as he portrays powerful and amazing relations with Israel's God. Once more the prophetic surfaces as the common denominator.

By the time David's reign is in full swing, the connection between God and His prophets is permanently forged. History has been made and Lord's archtype is forever set. From here on it is official, surely the Lord does nothing except He reveals His secret to His servants the prophets. Throughout scripture the prophets show up as the voice of God, the power of God exerted, and His weaponry. Hosea says as much when it says that the Lord hewns by His prophets. The most striking and telling account is that of the prophetic institution of Jezebel, the Phoenician witch King Ahab made queen of Israel. Her staff consisted of nearly a thousand prophets that she used to seduce, manipulate, and tyrannize the nation. She utterly usurped the Lord's messengers with her own and had the majority of them killed in order to stop their influence over her own institution. Solomon's prophetics show themselves in his receiving three personal visitations from God. At this point, things shift a bit as the kings are assigned prophets to serve their reigns. Jeremiah, Elijah, and the other major and minor prophets all continue the protocol up to and including the Lord Jesus Christ.

What all this says is that the occult, the supernatural, and witchcraft are all the reasons God maintains a prophetic staff. Elijah proves this point in his Mount Carmel clash with Jezebel's staff. The Lord shows apostate Israel that indeed her God really is the God of all gods, even though it was really too little too late. Nonetheless, our point has been made and that is that the prophet is God's arm, mouth, thoughts, and will. The reason is simple: the occult as we know it.

The word *occult* means "secret or mystical knowledge." It is a term embraced by witches, psychics, wizards, and sorcerers to identify the body of knowledge from which they gain their wisdom to exercise supernatural powers. Its relationship to the prophetic is obvious. It rivals the opposing wisdom, sensual and worldly, used against the Lord and His people. Branches of the occult, in addition to those stated above are divination, necromancy, astrology, magic, witchery, and sorcery. All are elements of the New Age religion that subscribes to polytheism, ancient mystical religions from the ancient Near East, and are condemned by Creator God. Being a supernatural and spiritual empire, the only godly counter to such powers and their forces are God's prophets. Church prophets need to know this because these agents are insidious in their infiltration of the modern church. For instance, yoga, a prime entrée to the occult, is pushed daily by the media and entertainment. Public schools peddle the ancient teachings under the guise of holistic wisdom, ignoring their religious and pagan roots. More than a few churches today subscribe to portions of this practice; overlooking its original aim to condition mediators to receive and embody the spirits of other gods. Many New Age practices are being supposedly helpful, healthy, and wholesome for today's frenzied world. Presenting them apart from their ritualistic and religious roots masks the roots and detriments of these teachings.

Of all the elements of the occult, divination is the most pervasive. It behooves prophets of the local church to understand divination. Its most pronounced treatment in scripture is Acts 16:16. Divination is simply speaking by the power of a fallen angel, devil, or demon. The definition alone tells why God has a problem with it. The divine in the word identifies the source of such words; psychics call them readings. In ancient times spirits were called divine beings because when they represented themselves to people they sought to enlist in their service and worship, they did so as gods—divine ones. Thus over time they were dubbed as divine ones and their words to humans as divining. Eventually, a supernatural institution developed around their visitations and communications that relied upon the hearer's performance of certain rituals. The collection of practices and rituals required to receive words from divine beings became known as divination. It rested on animal sacrifices, severed body parts, nature worship, and the handling of objects believed to possess magical powers deposited or designated by the interrogated deity as the mode of approaching and appealing to them for information. The information retrieved includes astrology, tarot and palm readings, crystal gazing, and necromancy, to name a few. Today, these are popularized as entertainment to hide their true aims.

Countless Christians call psychic hotlines to learn about their futures and to get advice from the supernatural about their life affairs. More than a few engage in talking to the dead, to ease the grief over a lost loved one. Millions follow their astrological sign and have their palms read. The psychic network is a multi-billion dollar industry that refuses to be curtailed no matter how many of its front liners are found to be charlatans. The hunger, better yet need, for answers to tomorrow drives people to do anything and pay any price to get even a tidbit of information. Such information for the Christian is locked up in the house of God in the prophets the Lord ordained to perform this function for His people. Having a prophetic staff in every church would release it and thereby discourage Christian temptation to seek the darkness for the light.

Chapter 11

Prophetic Job Description

Routine Activities of Church Prophets

This chapter of the book deals mainly with the local church prophetic institution. It gives further occupational details on the role and work of the church prophet. I have clearly established why the prophetic should be a functioning institution in the local church. Now that yours has been decided upon, here are some of its areas of operation.

The Prophetic in the Local Church

· Should be a full functioning institution.
· Should be under a prophetic superintendent.
· Should be a graduated appointment. Training and proving should precede placement on the team.
· Should only receive eligible appointees after trial period.
· Should have regular worship and congregational outlets.
· Should be assigned to various aspects of ministry for prayer coverage, insight, and spiritual watch care.
· Should be visibly represented in the local assembly.
· Should be replicating and outreach minded.

- Should have certified trainers and supervisors.
- Should require training and apprenticeship.
- Should encompass all spiritual activity.
- Should be under the church's school or learning department.
- Should develop and refine prophetic outlets for its ministers.
- Should arrange prophetic interaction and collaboration with other community prophets.
- Should be active in church's prayer, especially in its congregational prayer.

Prophetic Institution Staff Should Consist of the Following

- Prophetic types and prophets
- Intercessors and prayer warriors
- Special prophetic musical ensemble for psalmist
- Seers and church visionaries
- Prophetic trainers
- Prophetic mentors answerable to prophetic superintendent
- Staff prophets—*Well trained senior and junior ministers*
- Supervisory personnel over small units immediately answerable to superintendent and pastorate
- Superintendent of church prophetics answerable to senior pastor(s)
- A well trained force of competent prophetic voices.

Description of Church Prophet Activities

With their prophetic faculties, the resident or church prophet teaches the flock about God's ordained prophetics and helps them detect the true from the false. He or she trains the church to be responsive to the Lord and receptive to His Holy Spirit, paving the way for the pastor's actions, sermons, or announcements. It is through the church prophet that God expects to insure the church's accurate divine revelation in both spiritual and natural matters. The prophet then becomes the seasoned ears that try prophetic outbursts and the discerning eye that sift the false from the true. He or she is always alert to recognize emerging and awakening prophetic vessels in the congregation and prepared with a proven screening and training program to develop them.

Once budding prophets have been spotted, as with their ancient predecessors, the church prophet should be set to responsibly equip the newcomer to the office, and later qualify their credibility for service. Church prophets' superintending and training goals, considering this requirement, should be positioned to educate and supply prophets-in-training (PITs for short) to answer God's call. More than the ability to spiritually see something with their mind's eye and utter it should be required and their training should prove this. The ideal church prophet is interested in what smoothly integrates the new prophet to cultural life of the church. Master or chief prophets them should gear their PITs to serve competently when the time comes for them to be inducted into God's service. Their learning programs should implement every pedagogical method available to assure their success. Structured schooling then figures prominently in the constant ministry of the church prophet, or at least it should.

The work of a prophet in the local church, as you can see, is infinitely more involved than standing up in church and yelling, "thus says the Lord," and "I see a car, money, or home for you." Any psychic can do that. It is these other powers and functions that many prophets know little about, that distinguish the two.

Resident or staff prophets furthermore identify the lively stones, that is, potential workers, leaders, and ministers in the work and collaborate with the pastor on their development and installation. They further participate in the church's government as a subordinate or compeer ideally helping the shepherd order, structure, and maintain the house of God. Church prophets are key to their church's overall training aims and activities and instrumental to the success of its holistic spiritual stature in

Christ. Staff prophets are, furthermore, to be the sage counsel and the divine flow of wisdom pastors can look to for assistance in every godly way. They serve as one of the church's significant visionary pillars to validate and expedite the pastor's vision. This is important when the membership falls into skepticism or cynicism over a proposed venture or project the Lord wants the church to undertake. Zechariah and Haggai of old were prophets who performed this function. See Haggai 1 and Zechariah 1. Here is how they relate.

When the word came down from God to start rebuilding the temple and the wall of Jerusalem, the people were not at all motivated to do so. These two prophets stepped up and called on them to obey God's decree. They confirmed the word was of the Lord and supported the leaders practically, spiritually, and supernaturally in the project. Ezra 5:13 is one example of this. Prophet involvement guarded the work and backed it supernaturally to see that the vision of God did not veer off His designated course. So effective was the prophets' involvement, one wonders, considering Ezra and Nehemiah's conflicts during his work, if the task could have ever been done at all without them. Studying Ezra 6:14 shows how the passage strongly supports the exhortation in 2 Chronicles 20:20 concerning the ministry of the prophets. Nehemiah 6:7 enhances this phenomenon by underscoring God's use of His prophets to spiritually achieve anything significant He wants done.

A brief warning is indicated at this point. Do not overlook that these abilities are available to all prophets. Satanic prophets of the world do the same thing. They rely on their powerful prophet's spirits (Nehemiah 9:30) and divine covenants to achieve their diabolical ends. Nehemiah 6:14 alluded to this when he spoke of the prophetess Noadiah and the rest of the prophets sent against his effort to make him afraid and quite the task the Lord had assigned him. A name for the tactic is mercenary prophetics. Because they were paid to do so, Nehemiah's contemporaries repeated Balaam's error. They sold their gifts to the highest bidder and sought to exercise their authority to destroy a new work of the Lord's.

How can these extensive duties and functions of the church prophet be settled and employed by the pastor? They can by their prophets being thoroughly oriented in what the church needs and diligent in their spiritual watch. However, it must not be overlooked that great responsibilities carry with them corresponding privileges. To assure those privileges are balanced, pastors and church leaders must set limits on their church prophet's service and conduct regular evaluations and brainstorming sessions to make sure the ministry remains viable in the church.

Church Prophet limits

As said earlier, the prophet's authority in a pastor's church is strictly influential as delegated by the pastor. Church prophet limits, being set by the pastor, are subject to his or her revocation at any time. The resident prophet is not to displace the shepherd as head of the church in the eyes of the sheep. When there is a conflict that could harm or spoil the flock, the pastor has the final say (right or wrong). Prophets are to acquiesce to the pastor to spare the flock. If there is an irreconcilable difference, the prophet should move on, leaving the church and its headship intact. The prophet's anointing being the higher of the two means he or she can quickly overturn devilish attacks (should that be the case) and pray the Lord move upon the pastor's heart.

Identifying and Selecting Church Prophets

When it comes to pastors recognizing and ordaining church prophets, as has been said, great care should be taken. By now you understand that the person placed in the post should be a confirmed prophet and not a novice or a prophesier aspiring to the official post. Requiring church prophets to train for their posts, especially if they rose up from the pastor's flock, is wisdom. If a candidate for the position did not rise up from the pastor's flock, he or she should be ready to present reputable credentials to the pastor before being assigned to duty, and even then the assignment should be temporary until the prophet is proved. Submitted credentials should supply the pastor with the candidate's experience, background, years in prophetic ministry, and degree of training. The prophet's level of competence and skill for church prophet service should be stated in specific achievement and accomplishment terms. Also a service record and references for the pastor to check before installing someone as official church prophet should be made available. (This need not apply to prophets called in as guest ministers, but it is good policy.)

For church prophets there should be a trial period set to determine if they are compatible with the flock, its vision, mission, and perspectives. This requirement should become policy regardless of the number of years a candidate for the position of church prophet has been in prophetic ministry. It is common sense that protects the flock from prolonged discomfort or harm if the arrangement goes sour, and the Bible encourages it. For pastors considering authorizing prophets in their church, guidelines of this sort are more than practical, they are critical.

Requesting references may seem unpleasant or worldly to pastors, but they can prevent years of trouble. It is not secular to want to confirm the credibility and reputation of your prophet as a precautionary measure, it is actually quite spiritual as the Lord exhorts us to know those who labor among us (1 Thessalonians 5:12). As a matter of course, investigate more closely candidates who balk at this requirement to confirm their qualifications for the post. Sometimes a negative reaction may mean they have something to hide.

Furthermore, there is nothing wrong with asking for a background of the proposed church prophet's ministry covering any past engagements. Listen to a series of the prophet's messages on random dates before deciding their teaching is sound. You are looking for consistency in every professional area of the ministry.

The process for qualifying potential church prophets should include a thorough screening tool. This is recommended for verifying an incoming prophet's overall potential and for identifying the true prophet, and the prophet's truth. The screening used should consist of pointed questions that draw out informative answers about the prophet that pastors can use to base their decision upon. Such answers should provide insight into the candidate's prophetic vision for the church's covering and the means by which they propose to implement it. The questions posed should reveal the heart of the minister, his or her outlook on church prophetics, and their place in it. Naturally, doctrinal compatibility is crucial. The questionnaire you draft should tell you the proposed church prophet's spiritual and practical knowledge since teaching is likely to be a large part of their duties. How the prophet sizes up as a potential leader and matters of confidentiality and loyalty should all be addressed.

The Pastor and the Awakening Prophet

Should a pastor discover an awakening prophet in the congregation, the discovery should not automatically constitute an ordination, installation or appointment to church prophet. The most it should do is identify young prophets' calls and inspire novices to become trained and seasoned. Awakening does not of itself assure anointing, nor does it guarantee the quality of the awakening prophet's mantle, or its compatibility with the church and its vision. Prolonged observation of the novice's development is in order. For an exhaustive description of the traits and attributes that indicate the possible presence of a prophet's spirit, review previous chapters that profile prophetic character, abilities, and the like. To confirm the one you suspect may be prophetic or a prophet, assign a few ministry-related yet inconsequential tasks. Observe the person's handling of the tasks or resolution of assigned problems to be sure. This approach may be used by pastors to prove those who claim to be a prophet and to sift the mature from the marginal.

A critical factor to consider when dealing with an awakening prophet is the radical alteration of the relationship it causes between the prophet and the pastor. When this occurs many dynamic factors come into play that did not exist before. Relations between pastor and the member turned prophet may become strained now in ways previously unknown. The mandate given them both may clash. This could signal the prophet's call to another church when the reasons are not merely contention or resistance to change on both sides. All these considerations should be weighed carefully by the shepherd seeking to use a sheep turned prophet as the resident church prophet of a church.

Moreover when the office is installed in the church, the same safeguards and precautions used for other staff members should prevail with the church prophet in their churches. These precautionary measures should be cleared before the ordination ceremony. I cannot stress this enough. Pastors do not have to submit their flocks to untrained, inexperienced, or unverified prophets, nor should they be hesitant about requiring a proven track record from them.

Special Precaution

Pastors, be wary of lone prophets who have neither church accountability for their ministries, nor a reputable company of their peers to whom they voluntarily answer. Pastor, if a prophet has not come up under your ministry pastor, someone somewhere should be able to tell you about their prophetics and their ministry before you met them. Press for details of their ministry prior to releasing them in your church. Rigid reliance upon the Holy Spirit for revelatory confirmation of those you trust for prophetic ministry is acceptable. Nevertheless, it should be infrequent and not a routine substitute for reliable screening practices. The wisdom of God's word dictates this for the protection of the pastor and the church. I have learned over the years that when brothers and sisters in the Lord first meet each other their introduction is likely to be primarily spirit to spirit, and this is good. However, not all working relationships stay on that plane all the time. Therefore, pastor and prophet should want to get to know each other flesh to flesh, that is, the two of you may want to take time to get acquainted with one another's human sides.

The Church Prophet

You recollect how God awakens young prophets? That it is often in private which lends itself to immature prophet's resistance to established church authority. We talked much about this elsewhere. In this section we overview the chain of events that occur when God alerts a person that they are a prophet. It is not that the Lord's methods are wrong, but because of the darkness in humanity the early results can usually be unpleasant. Pride is always at the root of the human heart and the call to the prophet surfaces it quickly. That is what happens with new prophets.

Since young prophetic messengers get their starts from God in secret, they feel such a start means they are never to be in subjection to anyone but God. This attitude makes for turbulent times, as we have shown, and all too often ends with the novice prophet leaving the church and the frustrated pastor being left to deal with the wake of disaster they may have left behind. Meanwhile, the young prophet is most likely outside the camp of the Lord and away from the safety of the ark, so embittered and embattled is now wary of prophetics in the future. If there had been a medium between the two, the budding prophet and the busy and protective pastor, maybe things could have turned out differently. Perhaps the struggle that ended so badly could have been avoided. What would have happened if there were better ways to bring a new prophet up in the Lord?

One way to reduce the customary struggles between new prophets and their pastors is to direct awakening prophets to seasoned messengers that understand what they are going through who can help them learn their callings, their mantle, the ministry, and their place in the church. Here is where prophetic mentorship comes in.

The first thing all upset parties to a disorderly prophetic awakening should do is **not** throw out the baby with the bath water. Frequently, out of sheer frustration, that is the response of the typical church pastor. The prophetic on its own is a grave institution. Typically, those called to it are headstrong, strong willed, and independent, qualities that makes them good candidates for the calling in the first place. It fits the underlying prophetic nature and experience. Getting them off to a good prophetic start can be precarious. You see, prophetic types are accustomed to resistance. They are usually seasoned fighters, well able to isolate themselves and thrive in isolation. They easily adapt to the mood of their surroundings and deftly counterattack anything that threatens them. Prophets in general find it quite convenient to walk away from the crowd and to go against the grain of the masses. All these powerful tendencies, when sanctified, will make them good vessels of the Lord in prophetic ministry, but at the outset they are nerve wracking and quite destructive.

Seasoned prophets know this well. That is why they should be available for prophetic mentorship and established in the church as such. Prophetic mentorship means the burden of coping with a budding prophet is handed over to someone else, even if the pastor is a prophet.

The work of training, pruning, restraining, and trying the sincere novice is left on their shoulders. Once assigned, the prophetic mentor should make themselves available to their juniors for long talks, questions and answers, and other requirements of tutelage and training. A structured curriculum with teaching tapes and good books on the subject helps also.

The person usually assigned the prophetic mentor's function in the church is the church prophet. This individual in a small church generally doubles as the prophetic superintendent of the church. In large churches this is not necessarily the case, although the function may be delegated by the prophetic superintendent. Large churches are likely to have a staff of prophetic trainers assigned to this detail in the church. Whatever your structure pastors, anyone in the church feeling the call to the prophetic, or the awakening flames of the office of the prophet should be directed to the prophetic superintendent.

The Prophetic Superintendent

The prophetic superintendent should have on hand an established training program of coaching, counseling, and grooming methods to help their novices serve responsibly and harmoniously in the church. Their position should be publicized so church members know where to turn when they think their prophetics are being aroused. When they turn to the church's prophetic superintendent, they should be prepared to engage in a structured screening and preparatory process. There should be initial discovery tests: skills based activities and exercises, and evaluative systems that gauge their prophetic potential. After that placement becomes the issue as the prophetic trainer administers programs to foster their learner's growth, qualify, and strengthen their skills, and fortify their prophetic reliability. The goal of all teaching tools is the novice's maturity as a prophet. All prophetic learning and teaching processes should be well defined, and instructors should observe the students consistently for adjustment and confirmation of their success. The umbrella this prelude to prophetic readiness falls under is called mentorship.

Mentorship Is an Office

Mentorship of any kind in the Old World was understood as an official function. What made it so was the fact that parents, guardians, or other authority figures engaged mentors in a learner's life. In addition, mentorship was initiated because the learner was gifted and/or highly called and so in need of specialized training in order to succeed in that call. Mentorship assignments were given to knowledgeable representatives of the professional class or field, to which the learner was called, and identified by their skill and proficiency in their occupations. Not just anyone would dare to undertake the task of hanging out their shingle and enrolling students as a mentor. Mentors were highly respected as experienced and learned professionals of their fields—experts.

Mentors vastly differed from the typical educator. What they gave their students far exceeded mere academia. They distinguished themselves by the performance edge, skill advantage, and professional head start they gave their learners. The very things that qualified them as mentors are what benefited their students the most. As seasoned and successful professionals, mentors are identified as being well informed, well trained, and thoroughly exercised in their fields. Their well-documented skills and overall knowledge are considered to be far surpassing the majority of their contemporaries because of a proven track record. Mentor's expertise makes them able teachers and trainers because they effectively and profitably demonstrate their field's knowledge through competent instruction in the theoretical and technical aspects of their industry. Mentor's excel their learner's development with instruction and activities that go to the heart and soul of their student's potential and performance. Mentors inform, transform, and enable their learners to conform to the conduct, attitudes and behaviors of their fields.

Aims of Mentorship

As with any nurturing endeavor, there are concrete aims that regulate its activities and verify its success. With mentorship it is no different. Mentors initiate their services with specific ends in mind. Serious mentors are mindful of not allowing the agreement to become a mere social or servitude association. Following are some of the aims of a productive mentorship.

Quick Study Chart
Aims of a Good Mentorship

· Protection

- Preparation
- Instillation of valuable wisdom
- Fixed perspective of the field
- Internal creation of the instincts
- Allow manifestation of the skills
- Impartation of confidence
- Practicum
- Cultivate wisdom
- Skill development
- Mantle treatment
- Education
- Mentorship outcome

What to Expect from Mentorship

When you enter a mentorship, you should expect to be presented in your field, to showcase your mantle, promoted to your official calling. There should be some preliminary opportunities to work in the position you plan to occupy. Below are a series of Quick Study Charts to help you appreciate the parameters, guidelines, and benefits of mentorship from a professional and productive vantage point

Quick Study Guide
Important Mentorship Facts

- Mentorship is integral to all creation.
- Mentorship is an official function.
- Mentors should be educated in the field of ministry their mentorees are called.
- Prophets especially need to be mentored.
- Mentorships are to be mutually rewarding and mutually cooperative arrangements.

- Mentorship involves more than servitude.
- Mentorees should expect to have scheduled training, lectures, and development and be required to attend them.
- Mentor assignments should look to practical ministry functions and outlets.
- Mentorship relies on integrity, devotion, diligence, and loyalty.
- Mentorship must be formed with clear and honest motives and well defined objectives.
- Undeclared objectives and outcomes endanger the success of any mentorship.

Quick Study Chart
What Is Involved in Prophetic Mentorship

- Professional tutorials
- *Pneuma* academics
- Biblical scholarship
- Ministry business administration
- Occupational equipping
- Minister character development
- Mantle skills development
- Office competency training
- Supernatural prayer and spiritual warfare training
- Prophetic fluency coaching
- Kingdom and Christian communications
- People skills and people management training, interpersonal skills, and ministry relationships
- Problem solving and solution development
- Crises management and intervention
- Staff, worker, and volunteer management
- Fundraising
- Counseling and ministry execution

Quick Study Chart
The Uniqueness of Prophetic Mentorship

· Prophetic mentorship is unique compared to most mentorship agreements in that it is, of necessity, two dimensioned.

· Prophetic mentorship involves two-tiered treatment of the mantle: heaven and earth, eternity and time, spiritual and natural.

· Prophetic mentorship is an immutable standard for the Lord's true messengers.

· Prophets must be escorted to the realm of the spirit by a senior messenger if they are to be recognized and accepted as an authority in that sphere.

· The New Testament prophet must be mentored as well, even though the Lord Jesus is the Spirit of prophecy for them.

New prophets tend to be eager, somewhat overzealous, and overly reliant upon purely spiritual inflows and outlets for their early prophetic words. The ecstasy of the Holy Spirit becomes quite addictive to them as they seek to merely enjoy His sensations rather than His good sense. In the beginning, the idea of having a mentor is exciting. People seek it in much the same way as they look for a guru or a casual advisor. After they get one, their attitude changes. "When I need you, mentor, I will call you; otherwise leave me be and let me do my life and ministry as I see fit" becomes their unspoken intention. The real motive for wanting mentorship with these people is to brag that this or that one is my mentor. The idea of submitting to a mentor is rarely a factor in their minds.

However, those that realize that submission is a valid, invariable mentorship requirement tend to panic and dread it so much that they make matters worse when they come under their mentor's wing. They fear the structure, and shudder at the assignments, slack up on their service, or simply disregard the mentor's request, tasks, and lessons. To combat this temptation, here is an intelligent protocol of the spirit world that all prophets need to grasp and respect.

Coming Under Your Mentor's Wing
Coming under the mentor's wing can be intimidating in the beginning. Uncertain about what it will cost and require of you, you understandably feel a little frightened. Giving up control, letting another tell you what to do and virtually orchestrate your life is a bit unsettling. Once you do submit, you find it is much as you suspected it would be like, demanding and often ego breaking. It takes awhile for you to realize that it is also a power-shaping experience. For your mentorship to work, a clear-cut line of service, expectations, and requirements should be drawn.

In the beginning, and if you are serious, prepare to have little time for yourself. Initially you will be obliged to spend a large part of your life with your mentor, serving, learning, growing, and encountering. You will be stretched and that is the name of the game. But, if you want to get the best out or your mentorship, be guided by the following suggestions.

Quick Study Chart
Coming Under Your Mentor's Wing

- Be honest about your actions, reactions, motives, offenses, and defenses.
- Question your motives and honestly appraise your real self, especially in view of required mentorship duties.
- Explore your fears, doubts, anger, and resistance; particularly as they relate to authority figures.
- Ask yourself how selfishly motivated you may have been, or if you have a real problem developing in the area of difficulty that should be promptly handled?
- Are you really interested in being successful in God, and what will you sacrifice for it? Will it be pride, ego, and your indepen-

dence?

- What did you expect to get from and give to your ministry? Were your imaginations realistic.
- Now that you have given your word, are you going to back out or will you see through what you know the Lord called you to do?

In conclusion, the church prophet's job is demanding. Being the superintendent of a church's prophetics is even more so. Take a look at what are to be your duties and responsibilities to see how much the Lord is entrusting to you.

Quick Study Chart
Summary of Prophetic Superintendent Duties

Other Duties of Church Prophet Prophetic Superintendent Premise: Administration and Accountability for Stability

- Overseeing local church prophetics
- Collaborating with pastor and other ministers of the church of prophetic tenor and flow of the ministry
- Identifying and calling forth awakening and manifesting prophets in the congregation
- Working with and overseeing psalmists and seers of the church
- Leading church prophetic activities at home and throughout the community
- Installing or participating in the installation of leaders, new prophets, and such
- Attending to church's celebratory and commemorative events: baptisms, christenings, weddings, and the like
- Sharing pastoral visitation and similar loads as directed

- Establishing and confirming the office and function to which each prophetic officer belongs
- Administrating prophetic functions and supervising prophetic staff
- Arranging for prophetic outlets for prophetic members to service the body: conferences, classes, and special events
- Scheduling prophetic representation as desired by pastor for each church gathering
- Participating in, scheduling, and overseeing prophetic prayer and intercession in the church
- Augmenting normal church counseling with prophetic guidance and insight
- Identifying and disseminating quality prophetic material in the church
- Contributing to the church's fundraising and entrepreneurial ventures
- Standardizing church prophetic expressions
- Evaluating and ranking for use, emerging prophets
- Developing and acquiring curriculum for ongoing training and refinement of prophetic ministers
- Interacting with and submitting to the pastors needs and vision for the church's prophetics
- Scheduling and engaging outside prophetics and prophetic types to come in to minister to and refresh the church, its prophetic staff, and ministers
- Train, ordain, and cultivate novice prophets
- Correcting errant prophetics and prophetic excess in operation
- Screen prophetic actions and messages, often before they go forth to the body
- Standing and warring with pastor or church in spiritual conflicts

It is understood that the prophetic superintendent will have a staff to distribute these duties or delegate them as feasible. Just make sure the most sensitive responsibilities remain in his or her control.

When to Call in a Prophet

Much information has been given you on the subject of the prophetic in general and the church prophet in particular. You have been provided with background information on the ancient origins of the ministry and shown how it applies today. Nearly everything you need to institute the most efficient and effective prophetic order in your church and reap the fullest of benefits from it was included in this book.

The only issue not addressed so far is the use of the prophets in the local church apart from the church prophet's ministry. The Lord's persistent promotion of the ministry of the prophet means you who read this book will at one time or another receive a prophet into your church. It is scriptural to do so based on Matthew's record of Jesus' promise to reward those with like rewards for receiving His prophets. That being the case, the restoration of the office in mainline Christendom means most churches today and in the future will call in a prophet to minister the supernaturals of God on occasion. The question is how to know when to call one in.

Over the course of our discussions we have established how to know **who** to call in. What remains then is a means of deciding when a prophet should be called into your church to minister to your people. To begin to answer this question, I suggest you look back to the sections that dealt with the ministries of Zechariah and Haggai and their ministries to Ezra and Nehemiah. From that information alone you gain an idea of the situations that arise where you and your church can benefit from an itinerant prophet's service. Along with the examples given above, I want to add a few specifics that can help you make the decision on when to expose your church to prophetic ministry.

The first thing you may want to consider is any concrete voids your church may be currently experiencing due to lack of prophetic ministration. What are some of the humanist and demonic conditions surfacing or prevailing in your church? Can you, for instance, clearly see evidence of a spiritual attack or devilish infiltration on the wider population? Such assaults usually start at the head and generally target leadership first. The most diligent leadership can get weary or overwhelmed to the point their guard drops and the enemy takes advantage of their weakened state. So do not be reluctant to acknowledge the problems that surface, and by all means do not allow Satan to make you feel guilty or ashamed for needing some outside help.

Here are some examples of when to call in a prophet. We will start with marriages. Are the marriages in your church, especially the leaders', regularly dissolving all of a sudden? How about the youth? Is teen pregnancy rampant? Are drug addiction, criminal activity, and incarceration up among them? What about the physical health of the flock? Are sickness and disease, especially those of a debilitating or fatal sort, all too frequent? What about employment? Are your members' jobs constantly being lost and your sheep seeming to be the object of layoffs more than others? A yes answer to more than a few of these can signal a need for prophetic ministry in the church. However, there are others not as crucial but every bit as essential.

To illustrate, are you, the pastor, finding fewer and fewer financial or promotional breakthroughs experienced in the work overall? Is the fundraising down while the bills pile up? Do you encounter apathy and indifference from your people all too often, particularly in the area of money? Is the body at large afraid to give or enter into costly ventures with you? What about your ministers, trustees, elders, and leaders? Can you say they have been constant with you to date, or are you noticing a wavering indecisive trend regarding the moves you want to make? Are they confidently and competently handling, that is completing, their assigned projects, or are more and more of their duties going undone or being simply ignored?

How about their spirituality? Is there a steady progress in their ministry calls? Are they constant and diligent with the mandate of God on the church? Are they applying and growing from what they learn and therefore demonstrating effective in-church ministry? And then there are your church programs. Are the programs of the church flourishing or does it seem as if a bronze sky has replaced the earlier open heavens over you? Could you use a breakthrough in building negotiations, land purchases, zoning laws, or with the civil authorities in your area? Then any one of these reasons is enough for you to decide to call in a bona fide prophet.

To add to the above, consider the following. If your mandate has been changed or been completed and God is pressing you to do a new thing, then like Ezra and Nehemiah the time has come for you to add prophetic power to your normal church dispensation. Also, if there are frequent accidents, shortfalls, setbacks, or a powerful strangulation on the work of your ministry, a prophet is needed. In-fighting, leadership clashes, recent splits, spiritual harassment, and membership wandering too signal the need for prophetic power to restabilize your church. The major indication of all is death. If suddenly you find your membership hit often with the death of significant and stable members beyond the aged, a prophet is certainly needed in your church. Lastly, if there is a pressing need for huge financial infusions in the ministry you need a prophet with an economic stronghold in the heavenlies.

For additional guidance in this area you may contact:
Everlasting Life Ministries, Inc.
Tulsa, Oklahoma
For guidelines and surveys, address all correspondence to:
7030-C S Lewis Avenue, suite 468
Tulsa, OK 74136

GLOSSARY OF KEY TERMS AND PHRASES

1. **Agency**—An extension of an organization in a remote location authorized to transact business on its behalf.
2. **Agent**—An authorized representative of an organization.
3. **Biblical Prophetics**—Prophetics based on and operated in accordance with that described in the Bible.
4. **Church Prophet**—A prophet stationed in the local church.
5. **Commission**—A charge, calling, assignment, where delegated authority is given to a person or group dispatched to act on an organization, country, or company's behalf. Involves proxy, ambassadorship, and ministry.
6. **Divination**—Fortune telling and predicting by fallen angels.
7. **Divine**—The act of telling fortunes and predicting the future under the influence of an unclean spirit.
8. **Dreams**—Visual images that communicate to a sleeper.
9. **Feature and Functions**—Traits and their corresponding operations.
10. **Foundations Studies**—The basics of a subject or discipline.
11. **Functionary**—One who serves at the behest and on behalf of an authority.
12. **Mentor**—One who trains and nurtures another for a profession.

13. **Ministry**—Service to a deity or religion. May also be to a country or government.

14. **Mishmereth**—The watch duties and station of a prophet.

15. **Nabi**—An official prophet.

16. **Nastar**—The encircling effect of prophet covering.

17. **Office**—A position of trust, responsibility, and delegated or derived authority.

18. **Officer**—A person who occupies an office.

19. **Official**—The legitimate actions of an officer carrying out an office.

20. **Prophecy**—Saying what will or is to be before it happens.

21. **Prophet**—A spokesperson for a deity, one who invokes the gods.

22. **Prophetic**—That which proceeds from the prophet's work and authority.

23. **Prophetic Attributes**—That which characterizes prophets, revelations, and predictions.

24. **Prophetic Authority**—The rule, governance, and influence of the prophet.

25. **Prophetic Delegation**—Tasks, assignments, and authority received by prophets.

26. **Prophetic Function**—The professional operations of a prophet.

27. **Prophetic Guard**—A force of prophets assigned to a church for its spiritual protection.

28. **Prophetic Jurisdiction**—The spherical territory over which a prophet watches and governs.

29. **Prophetic Mantle**—The empowered cloak prophets of old wore to identify themselves as prophets.

30. **Prophetic Ministration**—The service and dispensation of a prophet.

31. **Prophetic Orientation**—Introductory teachings that expose and acquaint one to prophets and the prophetic.

32. **Prophetic Sphere**—A specific area of human and earthly existence over which a prophet has sway. Knowledge and information that com-

municate the disciplines of prophetic ministry.

33. **Church Prophet Superintendent**—The head of a local church prophetic organization.

34. **Prophetic Task**—Prophetic work, assigned by God.

35. **Prophetic Territory**—The physical and spiritual region of a prophet's clout.

36. **Prophetic Ward**—The literal station of a prophet's ministry, or assignment.

37. **Protocol**—A system of proprietary rules and precepts that govern activities.

38. **Protocratic**—Rulership of first founders or superseding authorities.

39. **Psalmist**—A singing prophetic, one who rhymes, sings predictions and revelations.

40. **Realm**—A designated area or division on earth.

41. **Seer**—One who sees what is ordinarily unseen by the natural eye.

42. **Sod**—Hebrew term for closed chamber deliberations of high powers.

43. **Sphere**—An invisible area or arena of dominance.

44. **Symbol**—An image or mark meant to signify something else.

45. **Territory**—A land division.

46. **Vision**—Images that communicate a message from unseen sources, or the mind.

BOOKS RESEARCHED
AND STUDIED

Genesis' Hebrew—Chaldee Lexicon of the Old Testament
H. W. F. Genesius
Published by Baker House Books, 1979

The Dictionary of Classical Mythology, Religion, Literature and Art
Oscar Seyfert
Published by Gramercy Books, 1995

Prophecy in Ancient Israel
J. Lindbloom
Published by Fortress Press, Philadelphia, 1965

Studies on Women at Mari
Bernard Frank Batto
Published by Johns Hopkins University 1974

The Hebrew Greek Key Study Bible
Spiros Zodhiates, Th. D.
Published by AMG Publishers 1984

Dictionary of Symbols
Jack Tresiddor
Published by Chronicle Books, Duncan Baird Publishers 1997

International Standard Bible Encyclopedia, Electronic Database
©1996 by Biblesoft

Nelsons Illustrated Bible Dictionary
Thomas Nelson Publishers 1986

The New Unger's Bible Dictionary
Moody Press of Chicago, Illinois, 1988

The Lost Books of the Bible and the Forgotten Books of the Bible
Published by LB Press, Cleveland, Ohio, © 1926

Other Books by Dr. Paula Price
God's Apostle Revived
The Apostle's Seminar
Constructing the Contemporary Prophet
The Five-Fold Officers of the Church of Jesus Christ
Prophetic Orientation
Biblical Prophetics—One
The Gifts of the Holy Spirit
The Prophet's Dictionary

ABOUT THE AUTHOR

Paula A. Price has been in active full-time ministry since 1985 with her husband, Tom, with whom she has three wonderful daughters and two grandchildren. Her ministry expertise includes pastoring three churches, founding and establishing a Bible institute with outreach and publication ministries and an international itinerant ministry. Today she pastors New Creation World Assembly in Tulsa, Oklahoma.

Before entering full-time ministry, Dr. Price was a sales and marketing account executive. Since then, she has become a writer and Christian educator developing curriculum to train Christian ministers and professionals in the wisdom of God. Paula blends ministerial and entrepreneurial applications in her ministry to enrich and empower Christ's churches' diverse skills and abilities. She sponsors retreats and seminars on a variety of Christian and Bible-based subjects, and has authored over 25 books, manuals, and courses on the prophetic, the apostolic, the five-fold ministries, Christian business and leadership, and a unique nearly-2,000 term *Prophet's Dictionary*. She also developed and teaches a unique local church course entitled "Prophetic Orientation" and hosts her own Christian talk show called "Let's Just Talk," where God makes sense. Her media experience includes regular guest hosting for a New Jersey live call-in radio show and hosting her own cable show for several years.

Her ministry goal is to effectively stabilize and increase Christian ministry service, applying God's wisdom and divine pragmatism to today's world solutions. Dr. Price seeks to make Christ's teachings and churches relevant today. Her ministry credo is "Eternity in the Now." Called an institute within herself, Dr. Price concentrates on maturing believers with information that profits and prospers, wisely taking you into the mind of God. She has a D.Min. and a Ph.D. in Religious Education from Word of Truth Seminary in Alabama.

Everlasting Life Ministries, Inc.

7030-C S. Lewis Ave
Tulsa, OK 74136
e-mail:
DRPAP1465@aol.com

Flaming Visions Publications
Books & Tapes Order Form

To order, call 1-866-305-0202 or FAX 405-216-0204

Customer Information

Name		Date		E-mail	
Address					
City		State		Zip	Office/Title
Phone		Church (optional)			

Qty	Item	Description	Price	Total
	Adventures in Prayer	A prayer manual designed for prophetic intercessors	$10.00	
	Best of Let's Just Talk	A 3-tape series that provides the most intriguing topics covered in the program	$14.00	
	Biblical Prophetics	An introduction to an intermediate course on the prophet's ministry as detailed in the Bible	$40.00	
	Church Prophets	Provides the key to understanding the prophet's role in the modern-day church	$15.95	
	Deliverance Series, The	A 6-tape healing series that brings you through the process of deliverance	$28.00	
	Destiny Through God's Prophets	An audio instruction series that prepares one for his or her prophetic destiny	$25.00	
	The Eternal Tithe	An audio teaching that explains the root of the tithe as an eternal covenant, not a religious tradition	$5.00	
	Local Church Prophetic Orientation	A course text for congregational prophetic training and development	$25.00	
	Mentoring Mentor	A discussion of the mentorship that describes the relationship and requirements between the mentor and the mentoree	$25.95	
	Prophetic Orientation Correspondence Course	A training and development course on the prophetic which includes live lectures and work text that be applied toward actual college credits	$35.00	
	Revelation of Revelation	A prophetic purview of the last book of the Bible	$26.95	
	Surmounting the Impossible	A powerful teaching packed into a 3-tape series that empowers you to conquer your obstacles and excel in God	$15.00	
	When I See the Blood	A teaching that delves into the life, intelligence, and power of the Blood of Jesus like you never heard before!!	$5.00	
	God's Apostle Revived	A 200+ page manual on the office of the apostle that goes beyond discussing the anointing and the giftings to describe the features and functions of the office and the character, temperament, and faculties of the officer.	$40.00	
	Biblical Prophetics	A 6-unit textbook and manual that guides teachers and learners through introductory prophetics. Suitable for formal classroom instruction, this text includes syllabi, assignments and exercises, practicum, and critical thinking	$40.00	
	The Five-Fold Officers	A thorough treatment of the Ephesians 4:11 officers that presents them as officials of the kingdom serving as Christ's representatives to His New Creation church on earth	$40.00	
			Subtotal $	
			Shipping & Handling $	$4.50
			Total $	

		Payment Method		
Check #	Drivers License		State	Exp.
Credit Card ☐ VISA ☐ Mastercard ☐ Discover		No. ☐☐☐☐☐☐☐☐☐☐☐☐☐☐☐☐☐☐☐☐		
Expiration Date	Authorized Signature			

Everlasting Life Inquiry Card

Name _____ Date _____

Address _____

City _____ State _____ Zip _____

Phone (_____) _____

I would like to receive information on (check area of interest)

- ❑ Books by Dr. Paula A. Price
- ❑ Tapes and Teaching albums
- ❑ "Let's Just Talk" TV Show (coming soon)
- ❑ Semester-in-a-Month Classes
- ❑ Local Church Prophetic Orientation Seminars (available at your church)
- ❑ Apostles Seminar
- ❑ Church Prophets Accelerated Training (taken from the Church Prophets Book—one-week module)
- ❑ Prophetic Retreat for Pastors, Leaders and Prophetic types only—four days of R&R
- ❑ To Set Up a School of the Prophets in Your Church or Community
- ❑ Elijah School of the Prophets (Oklahoma City, Oklahoma)
- ❑ To Put Your Name on Mailing List